Connected  Mathematics™

Blackline Masters
and
Additional
Practice

Grade 8

Prentice
Hall

Glenview, Illinois
Needham, Massachusetts
Upper Saddle River, New Jersey

ISBN 0-13-053131-6

2 3 4 5 6 7 8 9 10   05 04 03

Blackline Masters

and
Additional
Practice

for
Grade 8

This book contains blackline masters for the following units:

Thinking with Mathematical Models

Looking for Pythagoras

Growing, Growing, Growing

Frogs, Fleas, and Painted Cubes

Say It with Symbols

Kaleidoscopes, Hubcaps, and Mirrors

Samples and Populations

Clever Counting

Use the side tabs in this book to locate the desired unit. The page numbers listed match those of the pages in the back of the Teacher's Guide for that unit.

Blackline Masters

and Additional Practice

for *Thinking with Mathematical Models*

Problem 1.2 Follow-Up

For each graph, try to find a graph model that fits the experimental data as closely as possible. Compare your graph models with those drawn by others in your group. What strategies did you use to help you draw an appropriate graph model?

a.
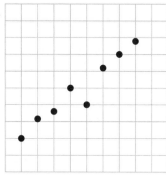

b.
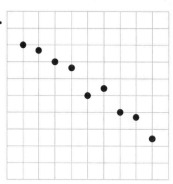

c.
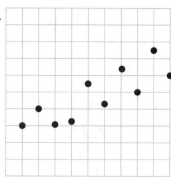

d.
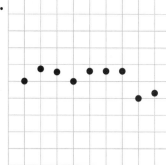

e.
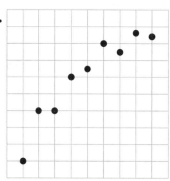

f.
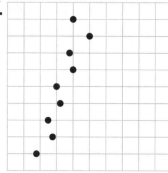

g.
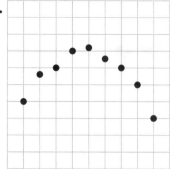

h.
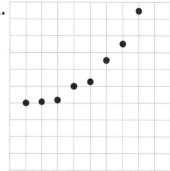

i.
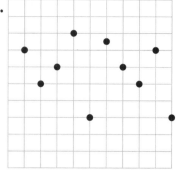

ACE Question 4

a.
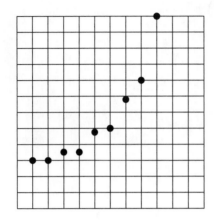

b.
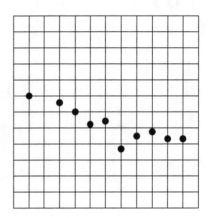

c.
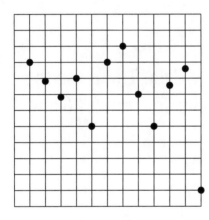

d.
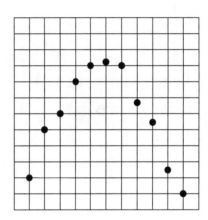

e.
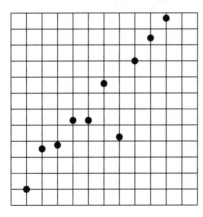

f.
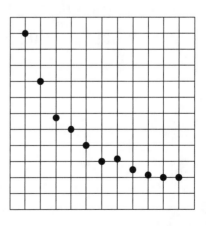

A. Do the bridge experiment to find breaking weights for bridges 1, 2, 3, 4, and 5 layers thick.

B. Make a table and a graph of your data.

C. Describe the pattern of change in the data. Then, use the pattern to predict the breaking weights for bridges 6 and 7 layers thick.

D. Suppose you could use half-layers of paper to build the bridges. What breaking weights would you predict for bridges 2.5 layers thick and 3.5 layers thick?

A class in Maryland did the bridge-thickness experiment. They combined the results from all the groups to find the average breaking weight for each bridge. They organized their data in a table.

Thickness (layers)	1	2	3	4	5
Breaking weight (pennies)	10	14	23	37	42

The class then made a graph of the data. They thought the pattern looked somewhat linear, so they drew a line to show this trend. This line is a good *model* for the relationship because, for the thicknesses the class tested, the points on the line are close to points from the experiment.

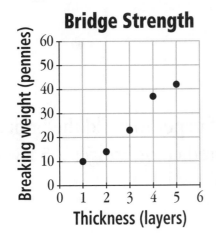

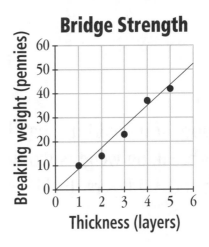

The line that the Maryland class drew is a graph model for their data. A **graph model** is a straight line or a curve that shows a trend in a set of data. Once you fit a graph model to a set of data, you can use it to make predictions about values between and beyond the values in your data.

© Prentice-Hall, Inc.

A. Draw a straight line that seems to fit the pattern in the (thickness, breaking weight) data you graphed in Problem 1.1.

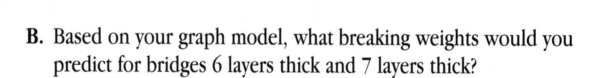

B. Based on your graph model, what breaking weights would you predict for bridges 6 layers thick and 7 layers thick?

C. Suppose you could use half-layers of paper to build the bridges. What breaking weights would you predict for bridges 2.5 layers thick and 3.5 layers thick?

Use a graphing calculator to explore the equation $y = 8.7x$.

A. Make a table of (x, y) data for $y = 8.7x$, using the x values 0, 1, 2, 3, . . . , 10. Explain how the entries in your table relate to the fact that $m = 8.7$ and $b = 0$.

B. Make a graph of $y = 8.7x$ for $x = 0$ to $x = 10$. Explain how the slope and the y-intercept of the graph are related to the equation.

C. What do the facts that $m = 8.7$ and $b = 0$ mean in terms of bridge thickness and breaking weight?

D. Solve the equation $60 = 8.7x$. What does the solution tell you about bridge thickness and breaking weight?

Price (dollars)	2	4	6	8	10	12
Number of buyers	400	325	230	160	100	25

A. Graph the (price, buyers) data, and draw a straight line that models the trend in the data.

B. Write a linear equation of the form $y = mx + b$ for your graph model.

C. What do the patterns of change in the (price, buyers) data and the graph model tell you about the relationship between the price and the number of buyers?

D. What do the values of m and b in the equation model tell you about the relationship between the price and the number of buyers?

E. Which data pair from the survey data is farthest from your graph model? Why do you think this point is so far from the graph?

Denise and Jonah earn allowances for mowing their lawns each week.

- Denise's father pays her $5 each week.

- Jonah's mother paid him $20 at the beginning of the summer and now pays him $3 each week.

The graphs of the relationships between the number of weeks and the dollars earned are shown below.

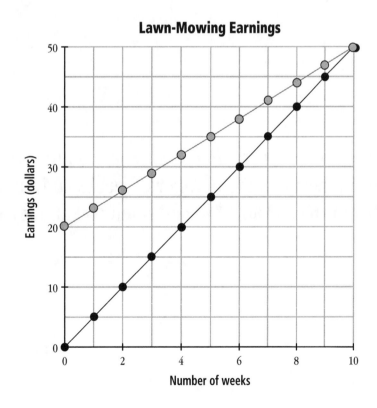

A. Which graph model shows Jonah's earnings as a function of the number of weeks? In other words, which shows how Jonah's earnings relate to the number of weeks? Which graph model shows Denise's earnings? Explain how you know which graph is which.

B. Write linear equations of the form $y = mx + b$ to show the relationships between Denise's and Jonah's earnings and the number of weeks.

C. What do the values of m and b in each equation tell you about the relationship between the number of weeks and the dollars earned? What do the values of m and b tell you about each graph model?

A. Find the breaking weights of paper bridges of lengths 4, 5, 6, 7, 8, 9, 10, and 11 inches. Organize your data in a table. Study the table, and look for a pattern. Do you think the relationship between bridge length and breaking weight is linear?

B. Make a graph of the (length, breaking weight) data from your experiment, and describe the pattern you see. Do the data appear to be linear?

C. Draw a straight line or a curve that seems to model the trend in the data. Do you think your graph fits the data satisfactorily? Explain.

D. Use your graph model to predict breaking weights for bridges of lengths 4.5, 5.5, and 6.5 inches. Make bridges of these lengths, and test your predictions.

E. How is the relationship between bridge length and breaking weight in this problem similar to and different from the linear relationships you studied in the last investigation?

A. Make a table of the (distance, weight) combinations you found. What does your table suggest about the relationship between distance and weight?

B. Make a graph of your data, and draw a straight line or a curve that models the trend. What does your graph suggest about the relationship between distance and weight?

C. How is the pattern of change in the (distance, weight) data similar to and different from the pattern of change in the (bridge length, breaking weight) data from Problem 2.1?

D. How is the pattern of change in the (distance, weight) data similar to and different from the pattern of change in the (bridge thickness, breaking weight) data from Problems 1.1 and 1.2?

A. Copy and complete the table to show the time it would take for the 300-mile trip at various average speeds.

Average speed (miles per hour)	30	40	50	60	70
Trip time (hours)					

B. Make a graph of the relationship between the average speed, S, and the time, T.

C. Find an equation for the relationship between S and T.

D. Is the relationship between S and T linear or nonlinear? Explain how the table, the graph, and the equation support your answer.

On Chantal's second birthday there was $116.64 in the savings account that Charlie had opened. The account has been earning 8% interest at the end of every year since Chantal was born. Charlie has not deposited or withdrawn any money since he opened the account. How much money is in the account on Chantal's fourteenth birthday?

A. If you started the experiment with 32 ounces of water in glass 1, how much water would be in each glass when you were done pouring? Arrange these (glass number, amount of water) data into a table. Describe the relationship between the glass number and the amount of water in the glass.

B. Make a graph of the data, and draw a straight line or a curve to model the trend.

C. Describe the pattern you see in your graph.

D. If you continued to add glasses and pour half the water from the last glass into the new glass, how much water would be in glass 20?

A. Tell which event each graph represents, and explain why you think the graph is a good model for the event. Copy each graph, and label the axes with the variable names.

1. 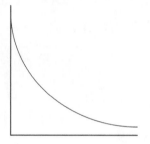   2.

B. Identify other events in the story that involve relationships between two variables, and sketch graphs that model the relationship between the variables. Carefully label the axes.

C. For each graph you sketched, write a sentence or two explaining what the graph shows and how it fits the description in the story.

D. Write a paragraph about the experiences a fourth group had. Sketch a graph or graphs that show how the variables in your story are related.

Graphs A–F show six possibilities for what might happen at some point after the passenger boards the bus. Each graph shows the relationship between time and distance from the bus station for the bus and the car. For each graph, make up a story about the bus and the car that matches the information in the graph.

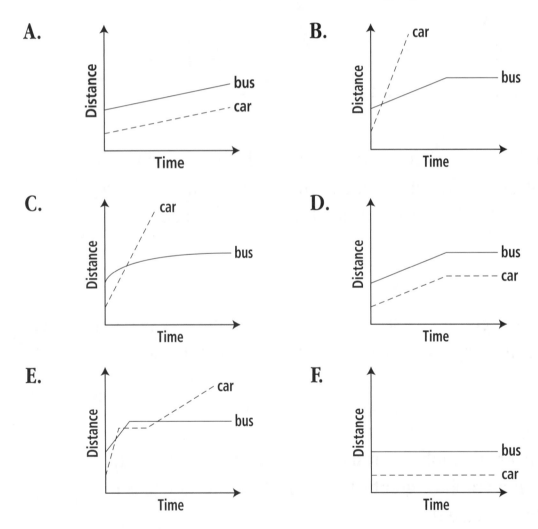

Which graph do you think best represents what might really happen? If none of the graphs seems correct, sketch a graph of what you think is likely to happen.

A. Use your calculator to graph each equation below. Adjust the window settings until you think you have a good view of the graph. Copy the graph onto your paper.

1. $y = \frac{1}{x}$

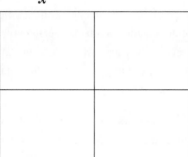

2. $y = (x - 1)(5 - x)$

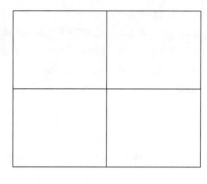

3. $y = 2.7x$

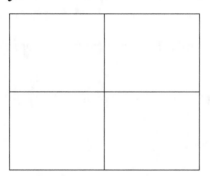

4. $y = 2^x$

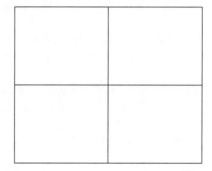

B. Choose two of the graphs from part a, and make up stories that could be modeled by them. For each graph you choose, be sure to tell which variable in your story is on the horizontal axis and which variable is on the vertical axis.

Dear Family,

The first unit in your child's course of study in mathematics class this year is *Thinking with Mathematical Models.* In previous mathematics work, your child has studied some of the basic concepts of algebra. In this unit, we will be exploring a variety of situations that can be represented with different mathematical models, including graphs and equations.

Students will conduct several experiments in this unit. One of the experiments simulates the work of structural engineers: students will test the strength of bridges made from paper, seeing how the strength changes as the bridges increase in thickness or in length. They look at different ways to work with the data they generate: displaying the data in tables, making graphs from the data, and sometimes writing equations to reflect what is seen in graphs.

Students will make graphs by plotting points on grid paper and by using graphing calculators. Graphing calculators enable students to make graphs more quickly and to explore many types of graphs more efficiently than is possible by hand.

You might help your child during this unit by observing tables and graphs in newspapers and magazines, and talking with your child about how they are used. Here are some other strategies for helping your child work with the ideas in this unit:

- Talk about situations in which data might be collected to help represent the situations with mathematical models such as tables and graphs.

- Look at your child's mathematics notebook. You may want to review some of the explanations that have been written for new concepts.

- Encourage your child's efforts in completing all homework assignments.

If you have any questions or concerns about this unit or your child's progress in the class, please feel free to call. We are interested in your child's success in mathematics.

Sincerely,

Estimada familia,

La primera unidad del curso de matemáticas para este año de su niño o niña se llama *Thinking with Mathematical Models* (El Pensamiento Puede Seguir Modelos Matemáticos). Antes de esto, su niño o niña ha estudiado conceptos básicos de álgebra. En esta unidad, vamos a explorar juntos una variedad de situaciones que se pueden representar con diferentes modelos matemáticos, incluyendo gráficas y ecuaciones.

Los estudiantes van a realizar varios experimentos. Uno de ellos consiste en simular el trabajo de ingenieros en estructuras; comprueban la fortaleza de puentes hechos de papel y ven cómo varía tal fortaleza de acuerdo al espesor o la longitud de los puentes modelos. Buscan formas distintas de trabajo según los datos que ellos generen: presentan sus datos en tablas, hacen gráficas con los datos, y a veces escriben ecuaciones que reflejan lo que se ve en las gráficas.

Los estudiantes harán sus gráficas marcando puntos en papel cuadriculado y usando calculadoras de graficación. Estas calculadoras les dan la posibilidad a los estudiantes de hacer gráficas más rápido y de explorar muchos tipos de gráficas con mayor eficacia que si lo hicieran a mano.

Ud. puede ayudar a su niño o niña durante esta unidad observando las tablas y gráficas que aparecen en los diarios y revistas y charlando con ellos o ellas sobre la forma en que se utilizan las mismas. A continuación les proponemos algunas otras estrategias que pueden ser de utilidad para apoyar a su niño o niña con el trabajo de la unidad:

- Converse con ellos o ellas sobre situaciones de las que se podrían recoger datos que sirvieran para representarlas con modelos matemáticos tales como tablas y gráficas.

- Hojee el libro de matemáticas de su niño o niña. Tal vez Ud. quiera repasar algunas de las explicaciones que se dan sobre conceptos nuevos.

- Aliente a su niño o niña a completar todas las tareas designadas para el hogar.

Si Ud. tiene alguna pregunta o preocupación sobre la unidad o sobre el progreso de su niño o niña, por favor no dude en visitarnos. Nos interesa que a ellos o ellas les vaya bien en matemáticas.

Atentamente,

Centimeter Grid Paper

Investigation 1

Use these problems for additional practice after Investigation 1.

In 1–4, write an equation and sketch a graph for the line that meets the given conditions.

1. A line with slope 3.5 and *y*-intercept $(0, 4)$

2. A line with slope $\frac{3}{2}$ that passes through the point $(-2, 0)$

3. A line that passes through the points $(2, 7)$ and $(6, 15)$

4. A line that passes through the points $(2, 1)$ and $(6, 9)$

In 5–8, write an equation for the line shown. Identify the slope and *y*-intercept.

5.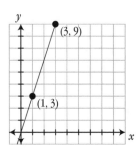

6.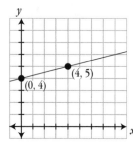

7.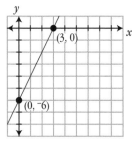

8.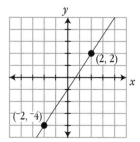

9. In a–c, write an equation and sketch a graph for the line that meets the given conditions. Use one set of axes for all three graphs.

   a. A line with slope $\frac{2}{3}$ and *y*-intercept $(0, 0)$

   b. A line with slope $\frac{2}{3}$ that passes through the point $(6, 6)$

   c. A line with slope $\frac{2}{3}$ that passes through the point $(6, 2)$

   d. What do you notice about the equations and graphs of the three lines?

10. In a–c, write an equation and sketch a graph for a line that meets the given conditions. Use one set of axes for all three graphs.

    a. A line with slope 3 and y-intercept $(0, 5)$

    b. A line parallel to the line drawn in part a with a y-intercept greater than 5

    c. A line parallel to the line drawn in parts a and b with a y-intercept less than 5

    d. What do you notice about the equations and graphs of the three lines?

11. In a–c, write an equation and sketch a graph for a line that meets the given conditions. Use one set of axes for all three graphs.

    a. A line that passes through *only* quadrants I and III of the coordinate grid.

    b. A second line that meets the conditions in part a

    c. A third line that meets the conditions in part a

    d. What do you notice about the equations and graphs of the three lines?

12. In a–c, write an equation and sketch a graph for a line that meets the given conditions. Use one set of axes for all three graphs.

    a. A line that passes through the point $(1, 8)$ and *only* quadrants I, II, and III of the coordinate grid.

    b. A second line that meets the conditions in part a

    c. A third line that meets the conditions in part a

    d. What do you notice about the equations and graphs of the three lines?

13. Consider the equation $y = 3x + 5$. In a–c, find the value of y for the given value of x.

    a. $(1, y)$ b. $(\frac{1}{3}, y)$ c. $(^-1.5, y)$

14. Consider the equation $y = 3x + 5$. In a–c, find the value of x for the given value of y.

    a. $(x, 0)$ b. $(x, ^-3)$ c. $(x, 1.5)$

Investigation 2

Use these problems for additional practice after Investigation 2.

In 1 and 2, write an equation and sketch a graph for the line that meets the given conditions.

1. A line with slope $-\frac{15}{5}$ that passes through the point $(-2.5, 4.5)$

2. A line that passes through the points $(2, -9)$ and $(-2, 3)$

In 3 and 4, write an equation for the line shown. Identify the slope and *y*-intercept.

3.

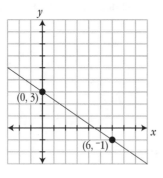

4.

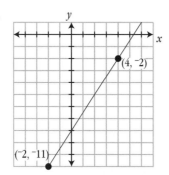

5. In a–c, write an equation and sketch a graph for the line that meets the given conditions. Use one set of axes for all three graphs.

    a. A line with slope -2 and *y*-intercept $(0, 0)$

    b. A line with slope -2 that passes through the point $(3, -3)$

    c. A line with slope -2 that passes through the point $(3, -9)$

    d. What do you notice about the equations and graphs of the three lines?

6. In a–c, write an equation and sketch a graph for a line that meets the given conditions. Use one set of axes for all three graphs.

   a. A line with slope $-\frac{1}{2}$ and y-intercept $(0, 3)$

   b. A line parallel to the line drawn in part a with a y-intercept greater than 3

   c. A line parallel to the line drawn in parts a and b with a y-intercept less than 3

   d. What do you notice about the equations and graphs of the three lines?

7. In a–c, write an equation and sketch a graph for a line that meets the given conditions. Use one set of axes for all three graphs.

   a. A line that passes through *only* quadrants II and IV of the coordinate grid

   b. A second line that meets the conditions in part a

   c. A third line that meets the conditions in part a

   d. What do you notice about the equations and graphs of the three lines?

8. In a–c, write an equation and sketch a graph for a line that meets the given conditions. Use one set of axes for all three graphs.

   a. A line that passes through the point $(-1, 8)$ and *only* quadrants I, II, and IV of the coordinate grid

   b. A second line that meets the conditions in part a

   c. A third line that meets the conditions in part a

   d. What do you notice about the equations and graphs of the three lines?

9. Consider the equation $y = -2x + 1$. In a–c, find the value of x given the value of y.

   a. $(x, 1)$ b. $(x, 5)$ c. $(x, -5)$

10. Here is one group's bridge-thickness data. This group used construction paper for their bridges.

Thickness (layers)	1	2	3	4	5	6
Breaking weight (pennies)	24	38	50	67	78	93

   a. Make a graph of the data. If appropriate, draw a line to show the trend and write an equation for the line.

   b. Predict the breaking weight of a bridge made from 14 layers of construction paper.

Investigation 3

Use these problems for additional practice after Investigation 3.

1. The graphs below show the results of four experiments. For each graph, do parts a and b.

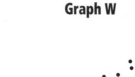

Graph W

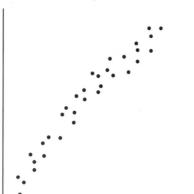

Graph X

Graph Y

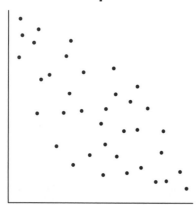

Graph Z

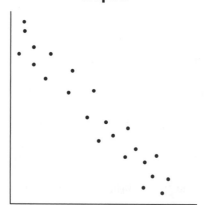

a. Describe the pattern you see in the graph.

b. If appropriate, describe the line or the curve you would draw to model the trend. If it is not appropriate to draw a line or a curve to fit the data, explain why.

2. In a–d, match the equation to a graph, and explain your choice.

    a. $y = -0.6x + 2$

    b. $y = 0.6x + 4$

    c. $y = -0.6x + 4$

    d. $y = 0.6x + 2$

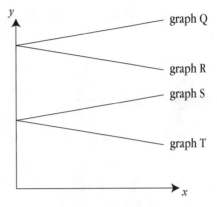

3. For each pair of equations in a–c, give the point at which their graphs intersect.

    a. $y = 3x + 2$ and $y = -3x + 2$

    b. $y = -2x - 1$ and $y = \frac{3}{4}x - 1$

    c. $y = \frac{3}{2}x - 7$ and $y = -3.4x - 7$

    d. What do you notice about the points at which the pairs of graphs intersect? Why do you think this is so?

4. In a–d, write an equation and sketch a graph for the line that meets the given conditions. Use one set of axes for all four graphs.

    a. A line that passes through the points $(0, -3)$ and $(3, 0)$

    b. A line that passes through the points $(0, 3)$ and $(3, 0)$

    c. A line that passes through the points $(0, 3)$ and $(-3, 0)$

    d. A line that passes through the points $(0, -3)$ and $(-3, 0)$

    e. At what four points do pairs of these lines intersect? What shape is formed by the line segments connecting these four points?

5. Batina did an experiment in which she grew bacteria. She collected these data.

Time (hours)	0	1	2	3	4	5
Number of bacteria	1	4	17	68	267	1036

    a. Make a graph of Batina's data, and draw a line or a curve to model the trend.

    b. Describe your graph model in words.

    c. What other situation have you seen that seems to have a similar graph model?

    d. Use your graph model to predict how many bacteria there were after 4.5 hours.

In 6–9, find the value of W or D that will balance the teeter-totter.

6.

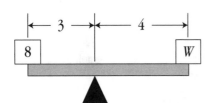

7.

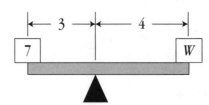

8.

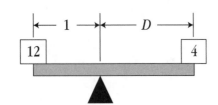

9.

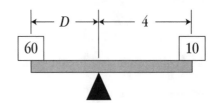

10. Suppose you are designing a rectangular garden with an area of 200 square feet.

    a. What perimeters can you make the garden using whole numbers? For each perimeter, give the length and the width.

    b. Suppose you know the length, L, of a rectangle with an area of 200 square feet. Write an equation that would help you to determine the width, W.

    c. Suppose you know the width, W, of a rectangle with an area of 200 square feet. Write an equation that would help you to determine the length, L.

Investigation 4

Use these problems for additional practice after Investigation 4.

In 1–4, sketch a graph and write an equation for the line that meets the given conditions.

1. A line containing the point (4, 2) and with slope $\frac{1}{4}$

2. A line containing the point (4, 2) and with slope $-\frac{1}{4}$

3. A line containing the point (4, 2) and with slope $-\frac{3}{2}$

4. A line containing the point (4, 2) and with slope $\frac{3}{2}$

5. Copy the diagram below, which shows graphs for four linear equations. Match each graph with an equation, and give reasons for your choices. Add sketches of the graphs for the two remaining equations.

    a. $y = 0.5x - 2$

    b. $y = 0.5x - 4$

    c. $y = -0.5x + 4$

    d. $y = 0.5x + 2$

    e. $y = 0.5x + 4$

    f. $y = -0.5x + 2$

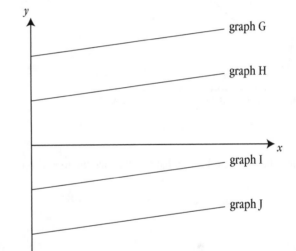

6. In a–d, write an equation and sketch a graph for the line that meets the given conditions. Use one set of axes for all four graphs.

    a. A line that passes through the points (0, −4) and (2, 0)

    b. A line that passes through the points (0, 4) and (2, 0)

    c. A line that passes through the points (0, 4) and (−2, 0)

    d. A line that passes through the points (0, −4) and (−2, 0)

    e. At what four points do pairs of these lines intersect? What are the slopes of the line segments that connect those points of intersection? Explain why this happens.

7. Write a story to fit this graph, which describes a race that Kate ran.

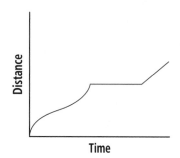

8. Write a story to fit this graph, which Emile drew to show how his hunger changed during a day.

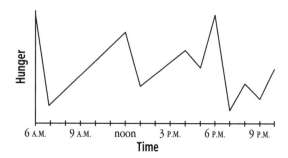

In 9–12, find the value of *W* or *D* that will balance the teeter-totter.

9.

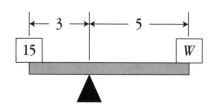

10.

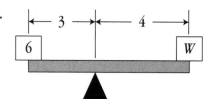

11.

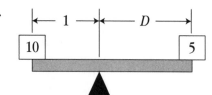

12.

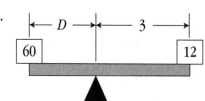

13. Suppose you are designing a rectangular garden with an area of 350 square feet.

    a. What perimeters can you make the garden using whole numbers? For each perimeter, give the length and the width.

    b. Suppose you know the length, L, of a rectangle with an area of 350 square feet. Write an equation that would help you to determine the width, W.

    c. Suppose you know the width, W, of a rectangle with an area of 350 square feet. Write an equation that would help you to determine the length, L.

    d. Make a graph using the equation you wrote in part b. Let x = length and y = width. Explain what your graph is showing.

14. Use only the first quadrant of the coordinate grid for this problem. If you are using a graphing calculator, set your window to show x and y values from 0 to 10 with a scale of 1.

    a. Graph the equation $y = \frac{10}{x}$ for x values from 1 to 10. For which value of x (from 1 to 10) is y the greatest? For which value of x is y the least?

    b. Graph the equation $y = 10x$ for x values from 1 to 10. For which value of x (from 1 to 10) is y the greatest? For which value of x is y the least?

    c. Compare the greatest and least values for y that you found in parts a and b.

    d. At what point do the two graphs intersect?

In 15–18, sketch a graph to fit the situation.

15. Joel started guitar lessons two months ago. He learned slowly at first, but his skill is increasing as time passes. However, he is going on vacation for two weeks and won't be able to practice at all!

16. Samantha ran a 10-kilometer race last weekend. She paced herself, running at a good but steady pace for the first 5 kilometers. She increased her pace during the next 4 kilometers. For the last kilometer, she was tiring but ran all out and managed to come in second.

17. Six friends decided to plant a garden. Glenda started planting the garden by herself, but she made slow progress. She had been working about an hour when two of her friends came along and helped her. After another hour, three more friends arrived to help. Glenda and the first two friends took a half-hour break while the three new workers got started, and then the six workers finished in another two hours.

18. Hani is riding his bike to see a friend who lives several miles away. For half an hour, he peddled pretty slowly, enjoying the scenery. Then, he noticed a dark cloud overhead. He increased his speed to try to outrun the rain. Ten minutes later the wind suddenly picked up. For about 20 minutes it was blowing in the direction he was going and then it turned directly into his face for the last 15 minutes.

Blackline Masters

and Additional Practice

for *Looking for Pythagoras*

Maps of Euclid

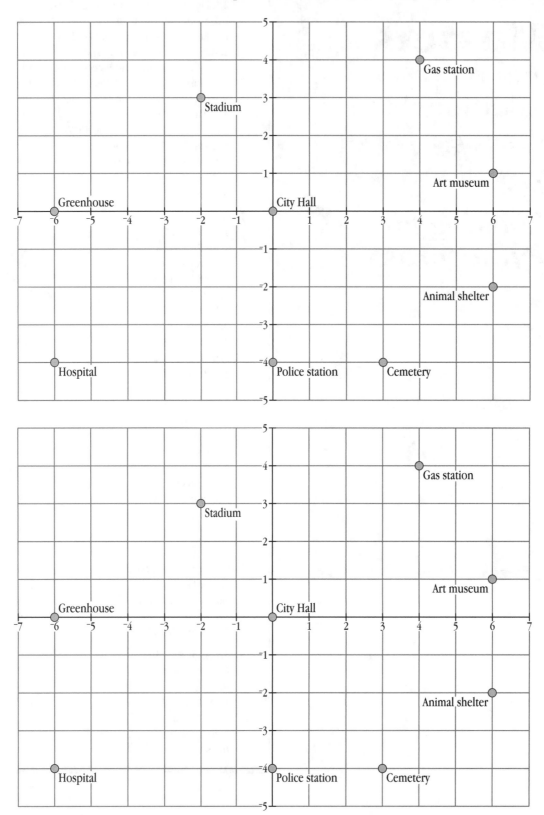

Figures for Problem 2.1 and Follow-Up

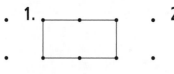

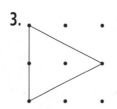

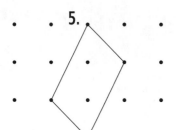

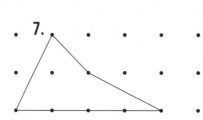

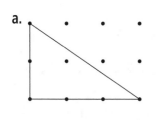

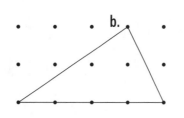

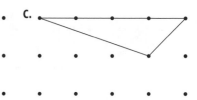

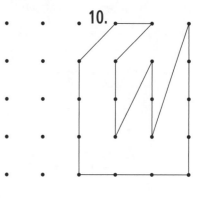

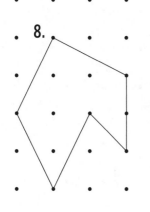

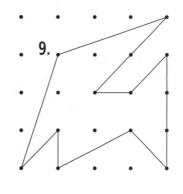

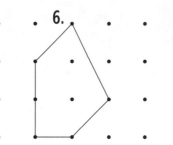

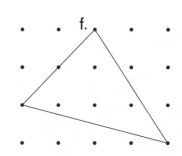

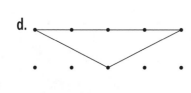

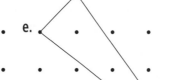

© Prentice-Hall, Inc.

5-Dot-by-5-Dot Grids

Enclosed 5-Dot-by-5-Dot Grids

ACE Questions 1, 2, and 11

Questions 1 and 2

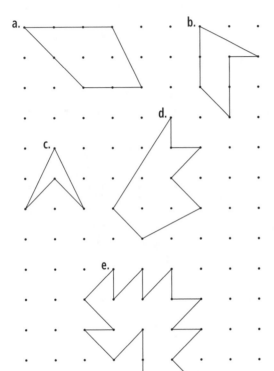

Question 11

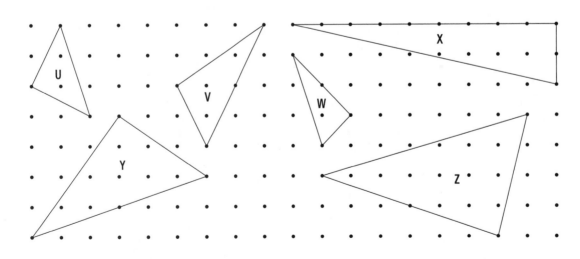

Puzzle Frames and Puzzle Pieces, Set A

Cut out the puzzle pieces. Arrange them to fit in the puzzle frames.

Puzzle frames

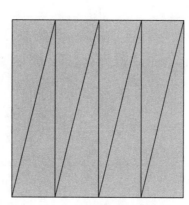

Puzzle pieces

Puzzle Frames and Puzzle Pieces, Set B

Cut out the puzzle pieces. Arrange them to fit in the puzzle frames.

Puzzle frames

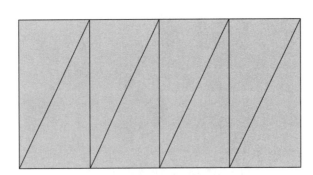

Puzzle pieces

Puzzle Frames and Puzzle Pieces, Set C

Cut out the puzzle pieces. Arrange them to fit in the puzzle frames.

Puzzle frames

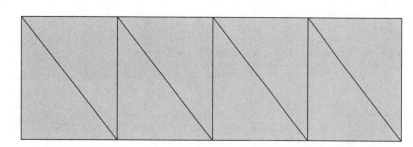

Puzzle pieces

Points on a Grid

Triangle and Square

Each side of equilateral triangle *ABC* has a length of 2.

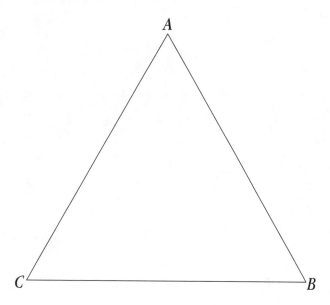 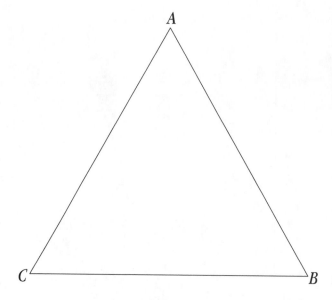

Square *ABCD* has side lengths of 1.

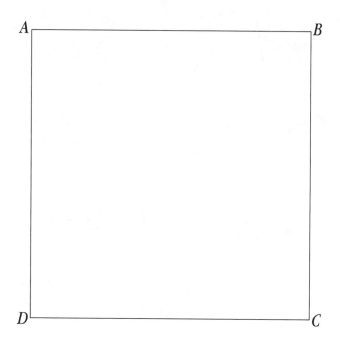 

The Wheel of Theodorus

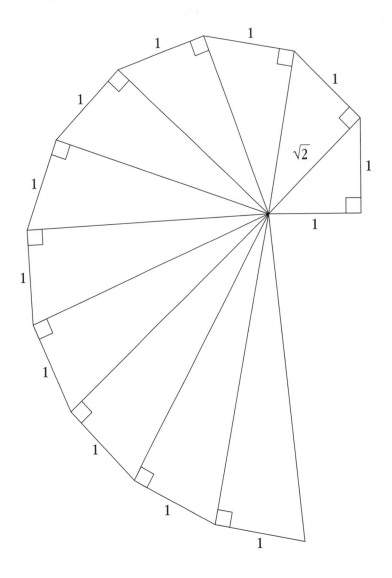

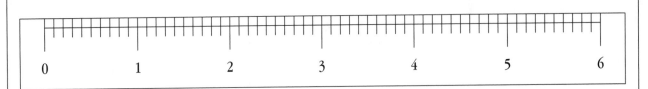

Escaping from the Forest

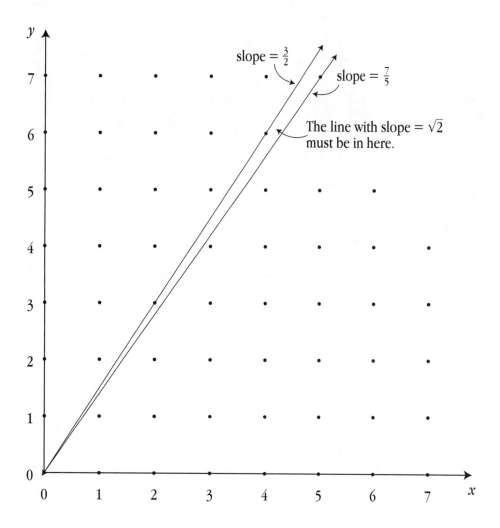

ACE Questions 1–6 and 15

Questions 1–6

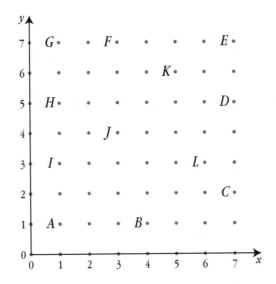

Question 15

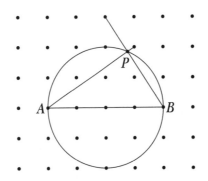

ACE Question 10

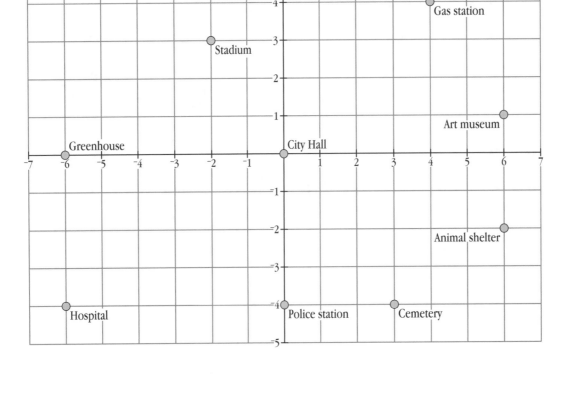

A. Give the coordinates of each labeled landmark on the map.

B. 1. How many blocks would a car have to travel to get from the hospital to the cemetery?

2. How many blocks would a car have to travel to get from City Hall to the police station?

3. How many blocks would a car have to travel to get from the art museum to the gas station?

C. How can you tell the distance in blocks between two points if you know the coordinates of the points?

© Prentice-Hall, Inc.

Your plan must include the shortest routes between the following pairs of locations. Answer parts A and B for each pair.

Pair 1: the police station to City Hall

Pair 2: the hospital to City Hall

Pair 3: the hospital to the art museum

Pair 4: the police station to the stadium

A. 1. Give the coordinates of each location, and give precise directions for an emergency car route from the starting location to the ending location.

2. Find the total distance, in blocks, a police car would have to travel to get from the starting location to the ending location along your route.

B. A helicopter can travel directly from one point to another. Find the total distance, in blocks, a helicopter would have to travel to get from the starting location to the ending location. You may find it helpful to use a centimeter ruler (1 centimeter = 1 block).

A. If the park with the given vertices is to be a square, what could the coordinates of the other two vertices be? Give two answers.

B. If this park is to be a nonsquare rectangle, what could the coordinates of the other two vertices be? Give two answers.

C. If this park is to be a right triangle, what could the coordinates of the other vertex be? Give two answers.

D. If this park is to be a parallelogram that is *not* a rectangle, what could the coordinates of the other two vertices be? Give two answers.

A. Find the area of each figure.

B. Describe the strategies you used to find the areas.

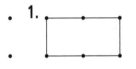

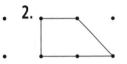

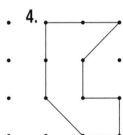

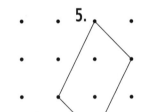

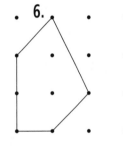

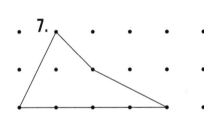

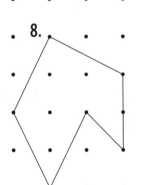

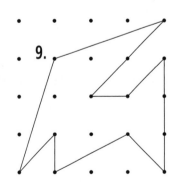

On the 5-dot-by-5-dot grids on Labsheet 2.2, draw squares of various sizes by connecting dots. Try to draw squares with as many different areas as possible. Label each square with its area.

© Prentice-Hall, Inc.

On the 5-dot-by-5-dot grids on Labsheet 2.3, draw line segments of various lengths by connecting dots. Try to draw segments with as many different lengths as possible. Use the method described in your math book to find the length of each segment. To find some of the lengths, you will need to draw squares that extend beyond the 5-dot-by-5-dot grids. Label each segment with its length. Use the $\sqrt{}$ symbol to express lengths that are not whole numbers.

A. For each row, draw a right triangle with the given leg lengths on dot paper. Then, draw a square on each side of the triangle.

Length of leg 1	Length of leg 2	Area of square on leg 1	Area of square on leg 2	Area of square on hypotenuse
1	1	1	1	2
1	2			
2	2			
1	3			
2	3			
3	3			
3	4			

B. For each triangle, find the areas of the squares on the legs and on the hypotenuse. Record your results.

C. Look for a pattern in the relationship among the areas of the three squares. Use the pattern you discover to make a conjecture about the relationship among the areas.

D. Draw a right triangle with side lengths that are different from those in the table. Use your triangle to test your conjecture from part C.

A. Cut out the puzzle pieces from Labsheet 3.2. Examine a triangular piece and the three square pieces. How do the side lengths of the squares compare to side lengths of the triangle?

B. Arrange the 11 puzzle pieces to fit exactly into the two puzzle frames. Use four triangles in each frame.

C. Carefully study the arrangements in the two frames. What conclusion can you draw about the relationship among the areas of the three square puzzle pieces?

D. What does the conclusion you reached in part C mean in terms of the side lengths of the triangles?

A. **1.** Draw a line segment between points *A* and *B*. Draw a right triangle with segment *AB* as its hypotenuse.

2. Find the lengths of the legs of the triangle.

3. Use the Pythagorean Theorem to find the length of the hypotenuse of the triangle.

B. Use the method described in part A to find the distance between points *C* and *D*.

C. Use the method described in part A to find the distance between points *E* and *F*.

A. 1. Do the whole-number lengths 3, 4, and 5 satisfy the relationship $a^2 + b^2 = c^2$?

2. Form a triangle using string or straws cut to these lengths.

3. Is the triangle you formed a right triangle?

4. Repeat parts 1–3 with the lengths 5, 12, and 13.

5. Make a conjecture about triangles whose side lengths satisfy the relationship $a^2 + b^2 = c^2$.

B. **1.** Form a triangle with side lengths a, b, and c that do not satisfy the relationship $a^2 + b^2 = c^2$.

2. Is the triangle a right triangle?

3. Repeat parts 1 and 2 with a different triangle.

4. Make a conjecture about triangles whose side lengths do not satisfy the relationship $a^2 + b^2 = c^2$.

Horace Hanson is the catcher for the Humbolt Bees baseball team. Sneaky Sally Smith, the star of the Canfield Cats, is on first base. Sally is known for stealing bases, so Horace is keeping a sharp eye on her.

The pitcher throws a fastball, and the batter swings and misses. Horace catches the pitch. Out of the corner of his eye, he sees Sally take off for second base.

How far must Horace throw the baseball to get Sally out at second base? Explain how you found your answer.

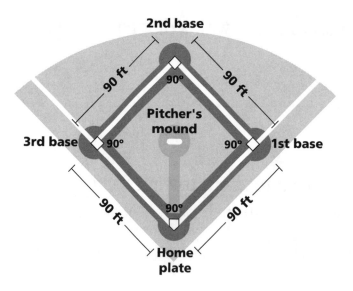

A. How does triangle *ABP* compare with triangle *ACP*?

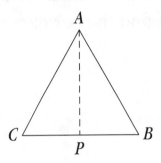

B. Find the measure of each angle in triangle *ABP*. Explain how you found each measure.

C. Find the length of each side of triangle *ABP*. Explain how you found each length.

D. Find a pair of perpendicular line segments in the drawing above.

E. What relationships do you observe among the side lengths of triangle *ABP*? Are these relationships also true for triangle *ACP*? Explain.

In the diagram below, some lengths and angle measures are given. Use this information and what you have learned in this unit to help you find the perimeter of triangle *ABC*. Explain your work.

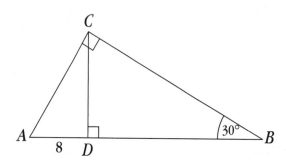

A. Use the Pythagorean Theorem to find the length of each hypotenuse in the Wheel of Theodorus. Label each hypotenuse with its length. Use the $\sqrt{}$ symbol to express lengths that are not whole numbers.

B. Cut out the ruler from Labsheet 5.1. Measure each hypotenuse on the Wheel of Theodorus, and label the point on the ruler that represents its length. For example, the first hypotenuse length would be marked like this:

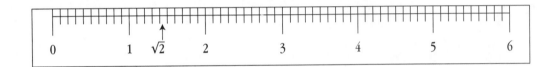

C. For each hypotenuse length that is not a whole number, give the two consecutive whole numbers between which the length is located. For example, $\sqrt{2}$ is between 1 and 2.

D. Use your completed ruler to find a decimal number that is slightly less than each hypotenuse length and a decimal number that is slightly greater than each hypotenuse length. Try to be accurate to the tenths place.

Write each fraction as a decimal, and tell whether the decimal is terminating or repeating. If the decimal is repeating, tell which digits repeat.

A. $\dfrac{2}{5}$

B. $\dfrac{3}{8}$

C. $\dfrac{5}{6}$

D. $\dfrac{35}{10}$

E. $\dfrac{8}{99}$

A. Copy the table, and write each fraction as a decimal.

Fraction	Decimal	Fraction	Decimal
$\frac{1}{9}$		$\frac{5}{9}$	
$\frac{2}{9}$		$\frac{6}{9}$	
$\frac{3}{9}$		$\frac{7}{9}$	
$\frac{4}{9}$		$\frac{8}{9}$	

B. Describe the pattern you see in your table.

C. Use the pattern to write a decimal representation for each fraction. Use your calculator to check your answers.

1. $\frac{9}{9}$ **2.** $\frac{10}{9}$ **3.** $\frac{15}{9}$

D. What fraction is equivalent to each decimal? Hint: The number 1.222 . . . can be written as $1 + 0.222$ . . . .

1. 1.2222 . . .   **2.** 2.7777 . . .

Caitlin is playing a video game in which she directs a character named Oskar through a series of obstacles. At this point in the game, Oskar is trapped in the center of an immense forest filled with trees planted in rows.

Oskar

The diagram shows part of the forest. Some of the laser trees have been labeled with letters, and *x*- and *y*-axes have been added. Oskar's location is labeled with an *O*.

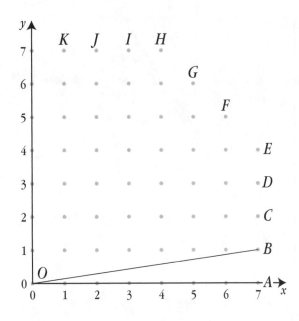

If Oskar had enough power, he could use a laser shield to walk right through the trees. Give the slope of the straight-line path he could follow to get from point *O* to each of the labeled trees.

The laser forest extends beyond the screen, but Caitlin is not sure how far. She wants to be sure Oskar won't hit a tree anywhere along his escape path.

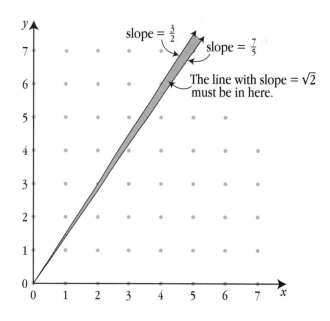

Study the drawing. On Labsheet 6.2, draw a straight-line path that Oskar could follow to get out of the forest. Give the slope of the path you find. Explain why you think your path will work.

Dear Family,

The next unit in your child's course of study in mathematics class this year is *Looking for Pythagoras.* This unit focuses on one of the oldest and most important relationships in all of mathematics, the Pythagorean Theorem. This is the relationship that says that in a right triangle, the sum of the squares of the lengths of the two legs is equal to the square of the length of the longest side, called the hypotenuse. Symbolically, this relationship is $a^2 + b^2 = c^2$, where a and b are the lengths of the legs and c is the length of the hypotenuse.

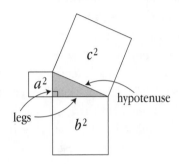

Students use this relationship to compute distances between points on maps and coordinate grids. They apply it to finding the lengths of line segments and other distances. For example, they use it to find out how far a helicopter travels from one point to another and how far a catcher must throw a baseball to get a runner out at second base.

Here are some strategies for helping your child during this unit:

- Ask for an explanation of the ideas presented in the text about finding distances. Help your child to find some examples of right triangles at home or in your community and to apply the Pythagorean Theorem to find the length of one side of a right triangle when the other two are known or can be measured.

- Discuss with your child how the Pythagorean Theorem is applied by people in some careers, such as carpenters, architects, and pilots.

- Encourage your child's efforts in completing all homework assignments. Look over the homework, making sure that all questions are answered and that explanations are clear.

As always, if you have any questions or concerns about this unit or your child's progress, please feel free to call. We want to be sure that this year's mathematics experiences are enjoyable and promote a firm understanding of mathematics.

Sincerely,

Estimada familia,

La próxima unidad del curso de matemáticas de su niño o niña para este año se llama *Looking for Pythagoras* (Busquemos a Pitágoras). Esta unidad está dedicada a una de las relaciones más antiguas y más importantes de las matemáticas, el Teorema de Pitágoras. El Teorema dice que en un triángulo rectángulo, la suma de los cuadrados de los catetos es igual al cuadrado del cateto más largo o hipotenusa. Simbólicamente, esta relación es $a^2 + b^2 = c^2$, donde a y b son las longitudes de los catetos y c es la longitud de la hipotenusa.

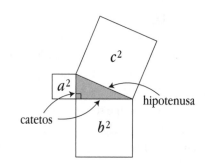

Los estudiantes usan esta relación para computar distancias entre puntos en mapas y cuadrículas de coordenadas. La aplican para hallar longitudes de segmentos lineales y otras distancias. Por ejemplo, para averiguar la distancia recorrida por un helicóptero entre un punto y otro o para saber cuán lejos un apañador debe tirar la pelota de baseball para lograr que el corredor quede afuera en la segunda base.

A continuación les proponemos algunas estrategias para ayudar a su niño o niña durante el desarrollo de la unidad:

- Pídales una explicación de las ideas presentadas en el texto sobre cómo averiguar distancias. Ayúdelos a encontrar ejemplos de triángulos rectángulos en casa o en su barrio y a aplicar el Teorema de Pitágoras para conocer las longitudes de uno de los lados del triángulo rectángulo cuando los otros dos son conocidos o se pueden medir.

- Discuta con su niño o niña cómo gente de diferentes carreras usa el Teorema de Pitágoras, por ejemplo carpinteros, arquitectos o pilotos.

- Aliente a su niño o niña a completar las tareas asignadas para el hogar. Revise sus tareas, asegurándose de que todas las preguntas han sido contestadas y de que las explicaciones son claras.

Como ya es habitual, si Ud. tiene alguna pregunta o preocupación acerca de esta unidad o acerca del progreso de su niño o niña, por favor no dude en visitarnos. Queremos estar seguros de que las experiencias dentro del campo de las matemáticas sean agradables para los niños y niñas este año, y también queremos promover una buena comprensión de la materia.

Atentamente,

Centimeter Grid Paper

Investigation 1

Use these problems for additional practice after Investigation 1.

Refer to the map on page 8 to answer 1–3.

1. Which landmarks are 5 blocks apart by car?

2. The taxi stand is 5 blocks by car from the hospital and 5 blocks by car from the police station. Give the coordinates of the taxi stand.

3. The airport is halfway between City Hall and the hospital by helicopter. Give the coordinates of the airport.

4. **a.** Draw a square with vertices (0, 1), (1, 0), (0, ⁻1), and (⁻1, 0). What is the area of this square in small triangles?

    b. Draw a square around the square you made in part a with two of the vertices at (1, 1) and (⁻1, 1). What are the other two vertices? What is the area of this square in small triangles?

    c. Draw the square of the next size. One of its vertices is (0, ⁻2). What are the other three vertices? What is the area of this square in small triangles?

    d. What are the four vertices of the square of the next size? What is its area in small triangles?

    e. What do you notice about the areas of the squares as the squares get larger?

    small triangle

5. Use the Venn diagram below to answer parts a–f. The Venn diagram shows a way to think about the classification of quadrilaterals.

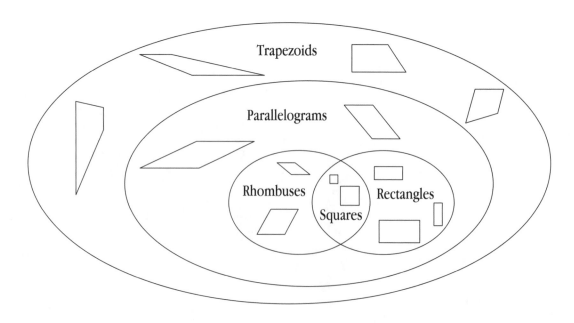

a. Which quadrilaterals have only one pair of parallel sides?

b. Which quadrilaterals always have four right angles?

c. Which quadrilaterals have two pairs of parallel sides?

d. *All squares are rectangles.* Is this statement true or false? If it is false, show an example that disproves it.

e. *Some rectangles are rhombuses.* Is this statement true or false? If it is false, show an example that disproves it.

f. *All trapezoids are rhombuses.* Is this statement true or false? If it is false, show an example that disproves it.

6. In parts a–d, draw the figure described. Recall that the sum of the angles in any quadrilateral is 360°.

a. Draw a quadrilateral in which at least two angles measure 90°.

b. Draw a rhombus in which at least one angle measures 45°.

c. Draw a trapezoid in which the angles measure either 40° or 140°.

d. Draw a parallelogram in which the angles measure either 40° or 140°.

In 7–12, use the given lengths to find the area of the figure. Show your calculations. Think about which formulas you can use as part of your reasoning.

7.

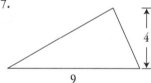

8.

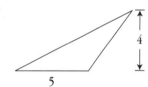

9.

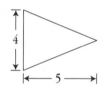

10.

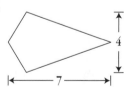

11.

12.

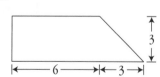

Investigation 2

Use these problems for additional practice after Investigation 2.

In 1–4, find the area of the figure. Describe the method you use.

1.

2.

3.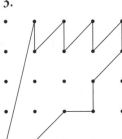

4.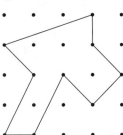

In Problem 2.3, you found the lengths of line segments drawn on 5-dot-by-5-dot grids. Some of those lengths were written as square roots, such as $\sqrt{2}$. When you enter $\sqrt{2}$ in your calculator, the result is a decimal with a value of approximately 1.4. In 5–10, find the approximate value for the given length to the nearest tenth.

5. $\sqrt{5}$

6. $\sqrt{13}$

7. $\sqrt{20}$

8. $\sqrt{17}$

9. $\sqrt{2} + \sqrt{5}$

10. $\sqrt{8} + 6 + \sqrt{10}$

11. Is $\sqrt{8} + \sqrt{10}$ the same as $\sqrt{8 + 10}$? Prove your answer in two ways:

    a. Use your calculator to help give a numerical argument.

    b. Use a grid and lengths of line segments to give a geometric argument.

In 12–14, find the perimeter of the figure. Express the perimeter in two ways: as the sum of a whole number and square roots, and as a single value after using decimal approximations to the nearest tenth for the square roots. An example is done for you.

The perimeter of this figure is $2 + \sqrt{10} + \sqrt{17} + \sqrt{5}$

$\approx 2 + 3.2 + 4.1 + 2.2$

≈ 11.5

12.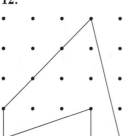

13.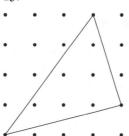

14.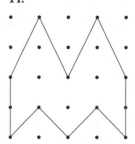

Use this information for 15–17: Triangles may be classified by angle measures or side lengths.

Classification by angles	Classification by side lengths
Acute triangle: all angles $< 90°$	*Equilateral triangle:* all sides same length
Right triangle: one angle $= 90°$	*Isosceles triangle:* two sides same length
Obtuse triangle: one angle $> 90°$	*Scalene triangle:* all sides different lengths

15. Recall that the sum of the measures of the angles in any triangle is 180°. There is one triangle listed above in which all three angles have the same measure. Which triangle is this? How did you decide?

16. Can you draw an isosceles right triangle on a 5-dot-by-5-dot grid? If so, draw one. If not, explain why not.

17. Can you draw a scalene triangle on a 5-dot-by-5-dot grid? If so, draw one. If not, explain why not.

In 18–21, copy the triangle. Use what you know about side lengths and angle measures to find the missing angle and side measures.

18.

19.

20.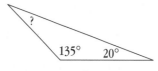

21.

Investigation 3

Use these problems for additional practice after Investigation 3.

1. Consider the right triangles shown below.

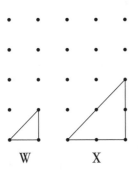 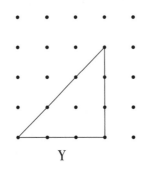 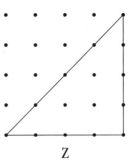

W   X   Y   Z

   a. Find the length of the hypotenuse of each triangle.

   b. How are the hypotenuse lengths in figures X, Y, and Z related to the hypotenuse length in figure W?

2. Draw a right triangle with a hypotenuse length of $\sqrt{5}$.

3. Draw a right triangle with a hypotenuse length of $2\sqrt{5}$.

4. Draw a right triangle with a hypotenuse length of $3\sqrt{5}$.

5. Give the coordinates of two points on a coordinate grid that are $\sqrt{10}$ apart.

6. Give the coordinates of two points that are $\sqrt{13}$ apart.

7. Give the coordinates of two points that are $\sqrt{32}$ apart.

8. Give the coordinates of two points that are $7\sqrt{2}$ apart.

9. Give the coordinates of a point on a coordinate grid that is a distance of $\sqrt{5}$ from point $(1, 3)$.

10. Give the coordinates of a point that is a distance of $\sqrt{17}$ from point $(0, -5)$.

11. Give the coordinates of a point that is a distance of $2\sqrt{5}$ from point $(-10, -2)$.

12. Give the coordinates of a point that is a distance of $3\sqrt{5}$ from point $(8, -2)$.

13. What is the length of the line that connects points $(0, 0)$ and $(4, 2)$?

14. What is the length of the line that connects points $(0, 0)$ and $(2, 4)$?

15. What is the length of the line that connects points $(-2, 0)$ and $(0, 2)$?

16. What is the length of the line that connects points $(0, -3)$ and $(3, 3)$?

In 17–19, find the perimeter of the figure to the nearest tenth.

17.

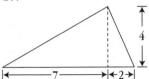

18.

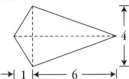

19.

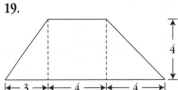

In 20–23, use the map on page 8 to find the distance by helicopter between the two landmarks, and explain how you found the distance.

20. the greenhouse and the police station

21. the police station and the art museum

22. the greenhouse and City Hall

23. City Hall and the animal shelter

In 24–26, find the perimeter of the right triangle. Express the perimeter in two ways: as the sum of a whole number and square roots, and as a single value after using decimal approximations to the nearest tenth for the square roots. An example is done for you.

The perimeter of this figure is $4 + \sqrt{10} + \sqrt{18}$

$$\approx 2 + 3.2 + 4.2$$

$$\approx 9.4$$

24.

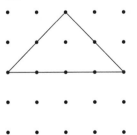

25.

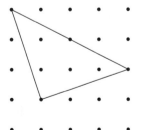

26.

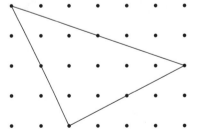

In 27–30, find the area of the figure. Describe the method you use.

27.

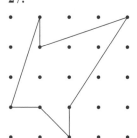

28.

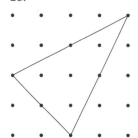

29.

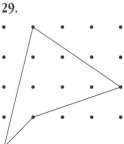

30.

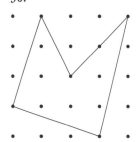

In 31–33, find the perimeter of the figure. Express the perimeter in two ways: as the sum of a whole number and square roots, and as a single value after using decimal approximations to the nearest tenth for the square roots.

31.

32.

33.

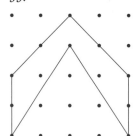

Investigation 4

Use these problems for additional practice after Investigation 4.

In 1–4, find the length of *AB* to the nearest hundreth. Show how you find the length.

1.

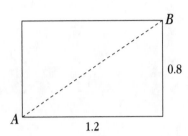

2. This is a regular pentagon.

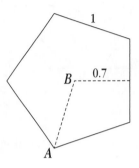

3.

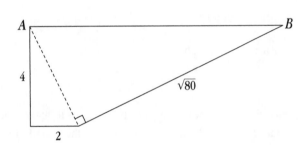

4. This is a regular hexagon.

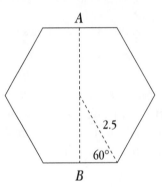

In 5–8, find the perimeter of the figure to the nearest tenth.

5.

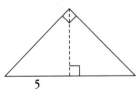

6.

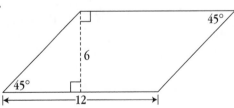

7.

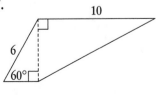

8.

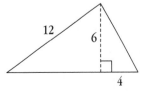

9. **a.** Find the areas of figures W and X. Describe the method you use.

   b. Draw two different figures Y and Z, each with an area of $7\frac{1}{2}$ square units. Be clever!

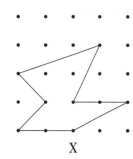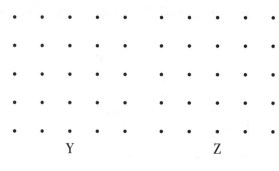

W   X   Y   Z

An isosceles right triangle has two legs that are the same length. In 10 and 11, sketch the triangle described, and label the three side lengths.

10. Two of the sides in this isosceles right triangle measure $\sqrt{18}$ and 3.

11. Two of the sides in this isosceles right triangle measure $\sqrt{52}$ and $\sqrt{26}$.

In 12–17, a pair of lengths are given. What third length could be used with the other two lengths to make a right triangle? Try to solve each problem two ways: (1) let the missing value be the length of one of the legs of the triangle and (2) let the missing value be the length of the hypotenuse of the triangle. Sketch each triangle you find, and label the side lengths.

12. 9, 15, and ?

13. 3, $\sqrt{45}$, and ?

14. $\sqrt{50}$, 5, and ?

15. $\sqrt{18}$, 3, and ?

16. 8, $\sqrt{18}$, and ?

17. $\sqrt{52}$, $\sqrt{26}$, and ?

Investigation 5

Use these problems for additional practice after Investigation 5.

1. **a.** What are the decimal representations of $\frac{1}{111}$, $\frac{2}{111}$, $\frac{3}{111}$, and $\frac{4}{111}$?

   b. Find other fractions with decimal representations the same as those of $\frac{1}{111}$, $\frac{2}{111}$, $\frac{3}{111}$, and $\frac{4}{111}$.

2. **a.** What are the decimal representations of $\frac{1}{33}$, $\frac{2}{33}$, $\frac{3}{33}$, and $\frac{4}{33}$?

   b. Find other fractions with decimal representations the same as those of $\frac{1}{33}$, $\frac{2}{33}$, $\frac{3}{33}$, and $\frac{4}{33}$.

3. **a.** What are the decimal representations of $\frac{1}{333}$, $\frac{2}{333}$, $\frac{3}{333}$, and $\frac{4}{333}$?

   b. Find other fractions with decimal representations the same as those of $\frac{1}{333}$, $\frac{2}{333}$, $\frac{3}{333}$, and $\frac{4}{333}$.

In 4–9, give a decimal representation of the fraction.

4. $\frac{43}{9}$ 5. $\frac{63}{99}$ 6. $\frac{1000}{333}$

7. $\frac{29}{11}$ 8. $\frac{290}{333}$ 9. $\frac{870}{999}$

In 10–12, give a fraction representation of the decimal.

10. $0.242424\ldots$ 11. $0.080808\ldots$ 12. $4.323232\ldots$

13. Name three fraction representations of the decimal $0.363636\ldots$.

14. In parts a–e, give the two consecutive whole numbers between which the given number is located.

   a. $\sqrt{17}$ **b.** $\sqrt{83}$ **c.** $\sqrt{250}$ **d.** $\sqrt{400}$ **e.** $\sqrt{1650}$

   f. How can you use your calculator to answer parts a–e?

In 15–18, tell whether the statement is true or false.

15. $7 = \sqrt{49}$ 16. $\sqrt{6.25} = 0.25$

17. $13 = \sqrt{149}$ 18. $\sqrt{777} = 27$

Investigation 6

Use these problems for additional practice after Investigation 6.

1. Find the slope of each line segment on the grid.

    AL   BL   KL   LD   IJ   JD   AJ   JE   GD   BD

2. Find each figure in the grid above, and match it with one of the names in the list. Names may be used more than once.

    a. figure *HGFD*
    b. figure *HJI*
    c. figure *FKE*
    d. figure *ABI*
    e. figure *ELC*
    f. figure *JKLB*

    Figures
    parallelogram
    scalene triangle (triangle with three different side lengths)
    trapezoid
    right triangle
    rectangle
    square
    isosceles triangle
    rhombus

3. Find the perimeter of each figure named in question 2. Approximate your answer to the nearest hundredth.

Blackline Masters and Additional Practice for *Growing, Growing, Growing*

Labsheet

Transparencies

Additional Resources

Additional Practice

Montarek Chessboard

A. Cut a sheet of paper as Alejandro did, and count the ballots after each cut. Make a table to show the number of ballots after 1 cut, 2 cuts, 3 cuts, and so on.

B. Look for a pattern in the way the number of ballots changes with each cut. Extend your table to show the number of ballots for up to 10 cuts.

Cuts	Ballots
1	2
2	4
3	
4	
5	
6	
7	
8	
9	
10	

C. If Alejandro made 20 cuts, how many ballots would he have? How many ballots would he have if he made 30 cuts?

D. A stack of 250 sheets of the paper Alejandro is using is 1 inch high. How high would a stack of ballots be after 20 cuts? After 30 cuts?

E. How many cuts would Alejandro need to make to have a stack of ballots 1 foot high?

A. Make a table showing the number of rubas the king will place on squares 1 through 16 of the chessboard.

Square	Rubas
1	
2	
3	
4	
5	
6	
7	
8	

Square	Rubas
9	
10	
11	
12	
13	
14	
15	
16	

B. How does the number of rubas change from one square to the next?

C. How many rubas will be on square 20? On square 30? On square 64?

D. What is the first square on which the king will place at least 1 million rubas?

E. If a Montarek ruba had the value of a U.S. penny, what would be the dollar values of the rubas on squares 10, 20, 30, 40, 50, and 60?

A. Plan 1 is the reward requested by the peasant, and plan 2 is the king's new plan. Complete the table to show the number of rubas on squares 1 to 16 for each plan.

Square	Number of rubas		Square	Number of rubas	
	Plan 1	Plan 2		Plan 1	Plan 2
1			9		
2			10		
3			11		
4			12		
5			13		
6			14		
7			15		
8			16		

B. How is the pattern of change in the number of rubas under plan 2 similar to and different from the pattern of change in the number of rubas under plan 1?

C. Write an equation for the relationship between the number of the square, n, and the number of rubas, r, for plan 2.

D. Is the total reward under the king's plan greater than or less than the total reward under the peasant's plan? How did you decide?

A. Make a table showing the number of rubas on squares 7, 8, 9, and 10 for plans 1 and 4.

	Number of rubas	
Square	Plan 1	Plan 4
7		
8		
9		
10		

B. For plan 4, write an equation for the relationship between the number of the square, n, and the number of rubas, r. How is this equation similar to the equation for plan 1? How is it different?

C. For plans 1 and 4, how many rubas would be on square 20? How many rubas would be on square 30?

D. Write a paragraph explaining why the peasant should or should not accept the king's new offer.

A. Make a table showing the number of rubas on squares 5 to 16 for the queen's new plan.

Square	Number of rubas
5	
6	
7	
8	
9	
10	
11	
12	
13	
14	
15	
16	

B. Write an equation for the relationship between the number of the square, n, and the number of rubas, r, for the queen's new plan.

C. Write a paragraph explaining why the peasant should or should not accept the queen's offer.

Look at the pattern in (day, mold area) data.

Day	Mold area (cm^2)
0 (start)	1
1	3
2	9
3	27
4	81

A. Describe how the mold area changes from one day to the next.

B. Write an equation for the mold area, *A*, after *d* days.

C. How is your answer to part A reflected in your equation?

Time (years)	Rabbit population
0	100
1	180
2	325
3	580
4	1050

A. The table shows that the rabbit population grows exponentially. What is the growth factor for this rabbit population? The growth factor from one year to the next is the fraction:

$$\frac{\text{population for year } n}{\text{population for year } n-1}$$

To find an approximate overall growth factor, compute the growth factors between several pairs of consecutive years and average your results.

B. If this growth pattern had continued, how many rabbits would there have been after 10 years? After 25 years? After 50 years?

C. How many years would it have taken the rabbit population to exceed 1 million?

D. Assume this growth pattern had continued. Write an equation you could use to predict the rabbit population, P, for any year, n, after the rabbits were first counted.

Assume that the value of Sam's coin collection increased by 6% each year for 10 years.

A. Make a table showing the value of the collection each year for the 10 years after Sam's uncle gave it to him.

Year	Value
1	
2	
3	
4	
5	
6	
7	
8	
9	
10	

B. For each year, find the ratio of the value of the coins to the value for the previous year. That is, find

$$\frac{\text{value in year } n}{\text{value in year } n-1}$$

This ratio is the growth factor.

C. Suppose the value of the coins increased by 4% each year instead of 6%.

   1. Make a table showing the value of the collection each year for the 10 years after Sam's uncle gave it to him.

Year	Value
1	
2	
3	
4	
5	
6	
7	
8	
9	
10	

   2. Find the growth factor by examining successive values in the table.

D. What would the growth factor be if the value increased by 5% each year? Explain your answer.

Sam gave some of his coins to his sister to help her pay college expenses. The value of the remaining collection was $1250.

A. Suppose the value of the remaining coins increased by 4% each year. Make a table showing the value of the collection each year for the next 10 years.

B. Sam's friend Maya has a baseball card collection worth $2500. Add a column to your table showing the value of Maya's collection each year for a 10-year period if its value increased by 4% each year.

Year	Value of coin collection	Value of card collection
1	$1300.00	$2600.00
2		
3		
4		
5		
6		
7		
8		
9		
10		

C. Compare the values of the collections over the 10-year period. How does the initial value of the collection affect the yearly increase in value?

D. How does the initial value of each collection affect the growth factor?

E. Write an equation for the value, V, of Sam's $1250 coin collection after t years.

F. Solve your equation to find the value of Sam's collection after 30 years.

A. The sheet of paper Alejandro started with had an area of 64 in². Copy and complete the table below to show the area of a ballot after each of the first ten cuts.

Cuts	Area (in²)
0	64
1	32
2	16
3	
4	
5	
6	
7	
8	
9	
10	

B. How does the area of a ballot change with each cut?

C. How is the pattern of change in the area different from the exponential growth patterns you have seen in this unit? How is it similar?

Time since dose (hours)	Active medicine in blood (milligrams)
0	20
1	10
2	5
3	2.5
4	1.25
5	0.625
6	0.3125

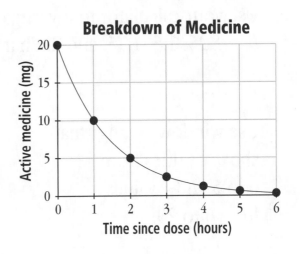

Breakdown of Medicine

A. How does the amount of active medicine in the dog's blood change from one hour to the next?

B. Write an equation to model the relationship between the number of hours since the dose was administered, *h*, and the milligrams of active medicine, *m*.

C. Based on your knowledge of exponential relationships, what pattern would you expect to see in the data if 40 milligrams of the medicine were given to the dog?

A. Use your calculator to investigate the equation $y = b^x$ for $b = 1.25, 1.5, 1.75,$ and 2. That is, investigate these equations:

$y = 1.25^x$ $y = 1.5^x$ $y = 1.75^x$ $y = 2^x$

Use window settings that show x values from 0 to 5 and y values from 0 to 20.

B. Use your calculator to investigate the equation $y = b^x$ for $b = 0.25, 0.5,$ and 0.75. That is, investigate these equations:

$y = 0.25^x$ $y = 0.5^x$ $y = 0.75^x$

Use window settings that show $0 \le x \le 5$ and $0 \le y \le 1$.

C. Based on your explorations in parts A and B, describe how you could predict the general shape of the graph of $y = b^x$ for a specific value of b.

Directions:

- Record the air temperature.
- Fill the cup with hot water.
- In a table, record the water temperature and the room temperature in 5-minute intervals throughout your class period.

Time (minutes)	Water temperature	Room temperature	Temperature difference
0			
5			
10			
15			
20			
25			
30			
35			
40			
45			
50			
55			
60			

A. Make a graph of your (time, water temperature) data.

B. Describe the pattern of change in the (time, water temperature) data. When did the water temperature change most rapidly? When did it change most slowly?

C. Add a column to your table. In this column, record the difference between the water temperature and the room temperature for each time value.

D. Make a graph of the (time, temperature difference) data.

E. Compare the shapes of the graphs.

F. Describe the pattern of change in the (time, temperature difference) data. When did the temperature difference change most rapidly? Most slowly?

G. Assume that the relationship between temperature difference and time in this experiment is exponential. Estimate the decay factor for this relationship. Explain how you made your estimate.

H. Find an equation for the (time, temperature difference) data. Your equation should allow you to predict the temperature difference at the end of any 5-minute interval.

Dear Family,

The next unit in your child's course of study in mathematics class this year is *Growing, Growing, Growing.* Your child has already explored a variety of relationships that can be represented with tables, graphs, and equations. This unit focuses on *exponential* relationships, in which a quantity grows larger or smaller at an increasing rate rather than at a constant rate.

Exponential relationships are often encountered in such fields as business and biology. We are dealing with *exponential growth* when we invest money in an account that earns compound interest or when we study population growth. We can see *exponential decay* in the way the body metabolizes medicine.

Your child has previously studied linear growth, in which a fixed amount is repeatedly added to a beginning quantity to produce a sequence of values. For example, in the sequence 2, 5, 8, 11, 14, . . . , each term is 3 more than the previous term. Exponential growth involves patterns that are based on multiplication rather than addition. For example, in the sequence 3, 9, 27, 81, 243, . . . , each term is 3 times the previous term. Students will learn to recognize exponential patterns in tables and graphs, and they will write equations to represent those patterns.

Here are some strategies for helping your child during this unit:

- Talk with your child about the applications that are presented in the unit and similar applications that you encounter in your daily activities.

- Discuss saving practices in your household. You might investigate with your child how investments, mortgages, or insurance policies involve exponential growth.

- Encourage your child's efforts in completing all homework assignments.

As always, if you have any questions or concerns about this unit or your child's mathematics program, please feel free to call. We are always pleased to talk with you.

Sincerely,

Estimada familia,

La próxima unidad del curso de matemáticas para este año de su niño o niña se llama *Growing, Growing, Growing* (Crezco un Poco cada Día). Su niño o niña ya ha explorado una variedad de relaciones que se pueden representar por medio de tablas, gráficas, y ecuaciones. Esta unidad se va a dedicar a las relaciones *exponenciales,* en las cuales una cantidad se hace más grande o más pequeña de forma creciente.

Generalmente, encontramos relaciones exponenciales en campos tales como los negocios y la biología. Estamos manejando un *crecimiento exponencial* cuando invertimos dinero en una cuenta que produce un interés compuesto o cuando estudiamos la población mundial. Podemos apreciar una *disminución exponencial* en la metabolización que hace el cuerpo de los medicamentos.

Antes de esto, su niño o niña ha estudiado el crecimiento lineal, en el cual una cifra fija se suma a una cantidad. Por ejemplo en la secuencia 2, 5, 8, 11, 14, . . . cada término vale 3 más que el anterior. El crecimiento exponencial implica modelos que se basan más en la multiplicación que en la adición. Por ejemplo en la secuencia 3, 9, 27, 81, 243, . . . cada término vale 3 veces el anterior. Los estudiantes aprenderán a reconocer los modelos exponenciales en tablas y gráficas y escribirán ecuaciones que representen esos modelos.

A continuación les presentamos algunas estrategias para ayudar a su niño o niña durante el desarrollo de la unidad:

- Converse con su niño o niña sobre las aplicaciones que se proponen en la unidad y sobre aplicaciones parecidas que Ud. encuentre en sus actividades diarias.

- Discuta con ellos acerca de las costumbres de ahorro en su hogar. Podrían investigar juntos cómo las inversiones, las hipotecas, o las pólizas de seguro se mueven de acuerdo a un crecimiento exponencial.

- Aliente a su niño o niña a completar todas las tareas asignadas para el hogar.

Como ya es habitual, si Ud. tiene alguna pregunta o preocupación acerca de esta unidad o sobre el programa de matemáticas de su niño o niña, por favor no dude en venir a vernos. Siempre nos complace charlar con Ud.

Atentamente,

Centimeter Grid Paper

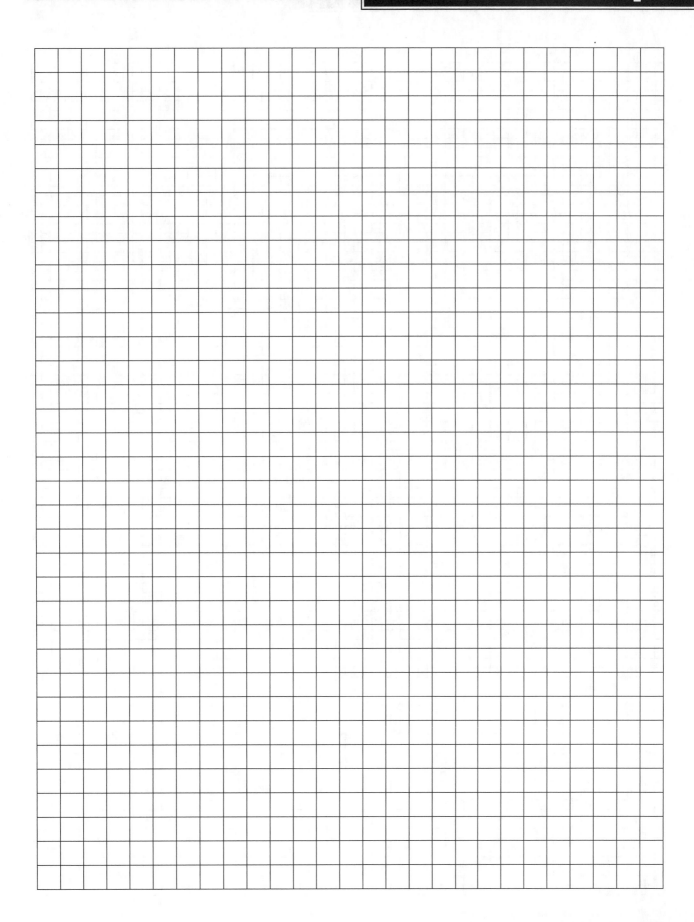

Investigation 1

Use these problems for additional practice after Investigation 1.

1. Cut a sheet of paper into fourths. Stack the four pieces and cut the stack into fourths. Stack all the pieces and cut that stack into fourths again.

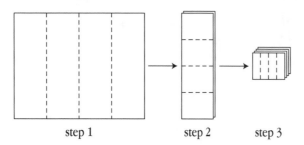

step 1   step 2   step 3

How many pieces of paper would you have at the end of

a. step 1?   b. step 2?   c. step 3?

d. step 10?   e. step n?

In 2–6, write the expression in standard form.

2. $2^0 \times 5^0$ 3. $2^1 \times 5^1$ 4. $2^2 \times 5^2$

5. $2^3 \times 5^3$ 6. $2^4 \times 5^4$

7. There are 64 volleyball teams entered in the state competition. In the first round of play, each team plays one other team, so 32 games will be played. The winners from these games play each other in a second round. The winners of the second round play each other in a third round. This continues until there is a final winning team. There are no tie games; games are played into overtime if needed.

a. How many *rounds of play* are needed before a winner is determined? Explain your reasoning.

b. How many *total games* are played before a winner is determined? Explain your reasoning.

c. Suppose an additional round of play is added to the playoffs. How many teams would start in the playoffs? Explain your reasoning.

8. Suppose you drew a pattern of branching lines starting with 3 lines:

Using a second color, you added 3 branches to the end of each of the first 3 lines:

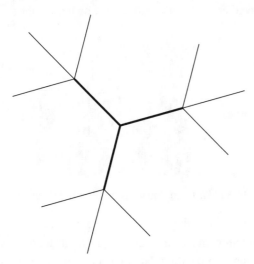

Using a third color, you added 3 branches to the end of each of the 9 new lines.

a. Copy and complete the table to show the number of branches you would draw in each new color.

Color	Branches
1	3
2	9
3	
4	
5	
6	

b. Write an equation showing the relationship between the number of branches drawn, b, and the number of the color, c.

c. What is the number of the first color with which you will draw at least 1000 branches?

d. Make a graph of the (color, branches) data from part a.

Investigation 2

Use these problems for additional practice after Investigation 2.

1. A bathtub is being filled at a rate of 2.5 gallons per minute. The bathtub will hold 20 gallons of water.

    a. How long will it take to fill the bathtub?

    b. Is the relationship described linear, exponential, or neither? Write an equation relating the variables.

2. Suppose a single bacterium lands on one of your teeth and starts reproducing by a factor of 4 every hour.

    a. After how many hours will there be at least 1,000,000 bacteria in the new colony?

    b. Is the relationship described linear, exponential, or neither? Write an equation relating the variables.

3. Two students who work in a grocery store are making a display of canned goods. They build a tower of cans 12 layers deep. The first layer, at the top, contains three cans in a row. The second layer contains six cans, in two rows of three that support the first layer. The third layer has nine cans, in three rows of three that support the second layer.

    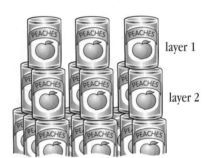

    a. How many cans are in layer 12, the bottom layer?

    b. Is the relationship described linear, exponential, or neither? Write an equation relating the variables.

4. An experimental plant has an unusual growth pattern. On each day, the plant doubles its height of the previous day. On the first day of the experiment, the plant grows to twice, or 2 times, its original height. On the second day, the plant grows to 4 times its original height. On the third day, the plant grows to 8 times its original height.

    a. How many times its original height does the plant reach on the sixth day? On the nth day?

    b. If the plant is 128 cm tall on the ninth day, how tall was it just before the experiment began?

    c. Is the relationship described linear, exponential, or neither? Write an equation relating the variables.

In 5–9, study the pattern in the table. Tell whether the relationship between x and y is linear, exponential, or neither, and explain your answer. If the relationship is linear or exponential, write an equation for it.

5.

x	0	1	2	3	4	5
y	2	9	16	23	30	37

6.

x	0	1	2	3	4	5
y	2	4	8	16	32	64

7.

x	0	1	2	3	4	5
y	$6\frac{1}{2}$	$8\frac{1}{4}$	10	$11\frac{3}{4}$	$13\frac{1}{2}$	$15\frac{1}{4}$

8.

x	0	1	2	3	4	5
y	500	1000	2000	4000	8000	16,000

9.

x	0	1	2	3	4	5
y	1	$\frac{1}{4}$	$\frac{1}{16}$	$\frac{1}{64}$	$\frac{1}{256}$	$\frac{1}{1024}$

Investigation 3

Use these problems for additional practice after Investigation 3.

1. Suppose you deposit $1000 in a savings account that earns interest of 6% per year on the current balance in the account.

    a. If you leave your money in the account for 10 years, what will the value of your investment be at the end of the 10 years?

    b. Is the relationship described linear, exponential, or neither? Write an equation relating the variables.

2. Janelle deposits $2000 in the bank. The bank will pay 5% interest per year, compounded annually. This means that Janelle's money will grow by 5% each year.

    a. Make a table showing Janelle's balance at the end of each year for 5 years.

    b. Write an equation for calculating the balance, *b*, at the end of any year *t*.

    c. Approximately how many years will it take for the original deposit to double in value? Explain your reasoning.

    d. Assume the interest rate is 10%. Approximately how many years will it take for the original deposit to double in value? How does this interest rate compare with an interest rate of 5%?

In 3–6, study the pattern in the table. Tell whether the relationship between *x* and *y* is linear, exponential, or neither, and explain your answer. If the relationship is linear or exponential, write an equation for the relationship.

3.

x	0	1	2	3	4	5
y	2	2.6	3.38	4.394	5.7122	7.42586

4.

x	0	1	2	3	4	5
y	500	550	605	665.5	732.05	805.255

5.

x	0	1	2	3	4	5
y	2.3	3.8	5.3	6.8	8.3	9.8

6.

x	0	1	2	3	4	5
y	1	4	8	32	64	256

7. Consider these three equations: $y = 5^x$, $y = 3^x$, and $y = 1 + 10x$.

    a. Sketch graphs of the equations on one set of axes.

    b. What points, if any, do the three graphs have in common?

    c. In which graph does the y value increase at the greatest rate as the x value increases?

    d. Use the graphs to figure out which of the equations is *not* an example of exponential growth.

    e. Use the equations to figure out which is *not* an example of exponential growth.

Investigation 4

Use these problems for additional practice after Investigation 4.

1. Joan and Jeff are standing 50 meters apart. They take turns walking toward each other. Jeff walks one half the distance between them, then Joan walks one half the distance between them. They take turns, each walking one half the remaining distance between them. Suppose that each walks 4 times (8 rounds) during this exercise.

   a. Make a table showing how far apart Joan and Jeff are after each of the first 8 rounds.

   b. Make a graph of your data from part a.

   c. Suppose that Joan and Jeff start over and take turns walking 3 feet toward each other. Make a table and a graph for this walking exercise showing how far apart they will be after each of the first 8 rounds.

   d. Compare the tables and graphs for the two situations. Explain the similarities and the differences you see.

2. A tree farm has begun to harvest a section of trees that was planted a number of years ago. The table shows the number of trees remaining for each of 8 years of harvesting.

Year	0	1	2	3	4	5	6	7	8
Trees remaining	10,000	9502	9026	8574	8145	7737	7350	6892	6543

   a. Assume the relationship between the year and the trees remaining is exponential. Approximate the decay factor for this relationship.

   b. Write an equation for the relationship between time and trees remaining.

   c. Evaluate your equation for each of the years shown in the table below to find the approximate number of trees remaining.

Year	10	15	20	25	30	35	40
Trees remaining							

   d. The owners of the farm intend to stop harvesting when only 15% of the trees remain. During which year will this occur? Explain your reasoning.

3. Consider these three equations: $y = 0.625^x$, $y = 0.375^x$, and $y = 1 - 0.5x$.

   a. Sketch graphs of the equations on one set of axes.

   b. What points, if any, do the three graphs have in common?

   c. In which graph does the y value decrease at a faster and faster rate as the x value increases?

   d. Which of the equations is *not* an example of exponential decay? Use the graphs or the equations to answer this question.

4. Tribetts are fuzzy insects that reproduce at the rate of 50% every day. Suppose you begin with 100 tribetts.

   a. Make a table showing the growth in the number of tribetts for the first 10 days.

   b. On what day will there first be 1000 tribetts?

   c. Write an equation for the relationship between days, d, and numbers of tribetts, T.

5. Suppose the number of tribetts in the fall of the year decreases at a rate of 30% per day.

   a. Make a table showing the number of tribetts at the end of each of the first 10 days for a starting population of 10,000 tribetts.

   b. Write an equation for the relationship between days, d, and number of tribetts, T.

   c. On what day will there first be fewer than 1000 tribetts?

Blackline Masters

and Additional Practice

for *Frogs, Fleas, and Painted Cubes*

Graphs for Problem 2.4

Graph 1

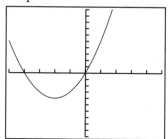

Graph 2

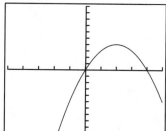

Graph 3

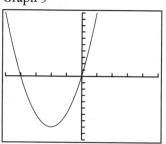

Graph 4

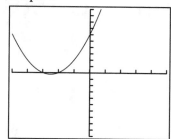

Graph 5

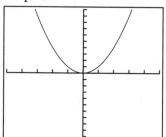

Graph 6

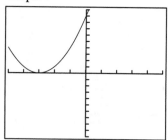

Graph 7

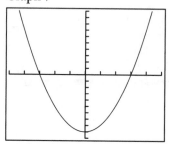

Graph 8

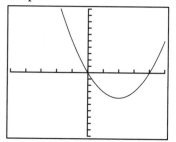

Tables for Problem 4.3

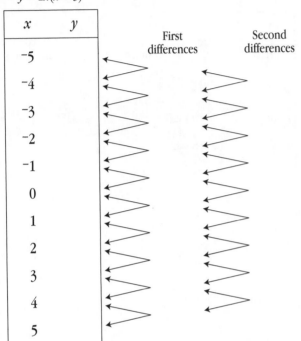

$y = 2x(x + 3)$

x	y
-5	
-4	
-3	
-2	
-1	
0	
1	
2	
3	
4	
5	

First differences   Second differences

$y = 3x - x^2$

x	y
-5	
-4	
-3	
-2	
-1	
0	
1	
2	
3	
4	
5	

First differences   Second differences

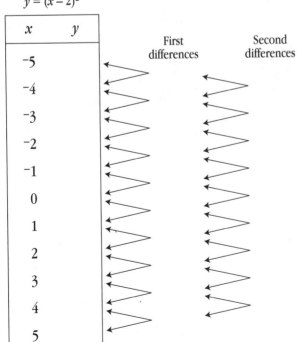

$y = (x - 2)^2$

x	y
-5	
-4	
-3	
-2	
-1	
0	
1	
2	
3	
4	
5	

First differences   Second differences

$y = x^2 + 5x + 6$

x	y
-5	
-4	
-3	
-2	
-1	
0	
1	
2	
3	
4	
5	

First differences   Second differences

Tables for Problem 4.3 Follow-Up

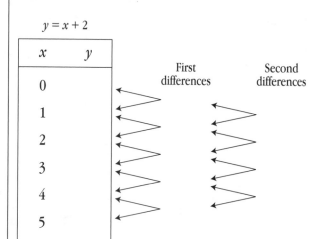

$y = x + 2$

x	y
0	
1	
2	
3	
4	
5	

First differences   Second differences

$y = 2x$

x	y
0	
1	
2	
3	
4	
5	

First differences   Second differences

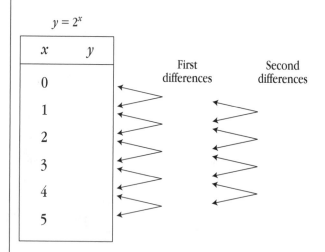

$y = 2^x$

x	y
0	
1	
2	
3	
4	
5	

First differences   Second differences

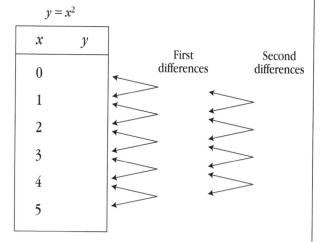

$y = x^2$

x	y
0	
1	
2	
3	
4	
5	

First differences   Second differences

Suppose the Mars colony adds the restriction that each claim must be rectangular.

A. Sketch several rectangles with a perimeter of 20 meters. Include some with small areas and some with large areas. Label the dimensions of each rectangle.

B. Make a table showing the length of a side and the area for each rectangle with a perimeter of 20 meters and whole-number side lengths.

Length of a side (m)	Area (m²)
0	
1	
2	

C. Make a graph of your (length of a side, area) data. Describe the shape of the graph.

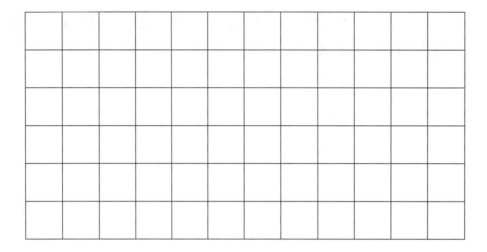

D. If you want to enclose the greatest area possible with your fencing, what should the dimensions of your fence be? How can you use your graph to justify your answer?

The graph below shows length and area data for rectangles with a fixed perimeter.

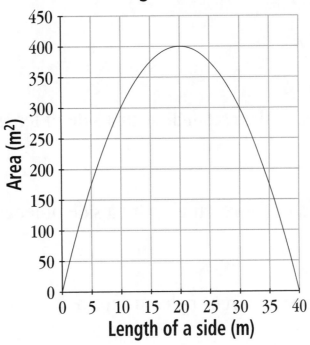

Areas of Rectangles with Fixed Perimeter

A. Describe the shape of the graph and any special features you observe.

B. What is the greatest area possible for a rectangle with this perimeter? What are the dimensions of this rectangle?

C. What is the area of the rectangle with a side of length 12 meters?

What is the area of the rectangle with a side of length 28 meters?

Explain how these two rectangles are related.

D. What are the dimensions of the rectangle with an area of 300 square meters?

E. What is the fixed perimeter for the rectangles represented by the graph? Explain how you found the perimeter.

Graph for a Linear Relationship

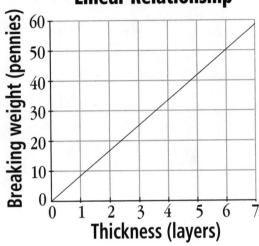

Graph for an Exponential Relationship

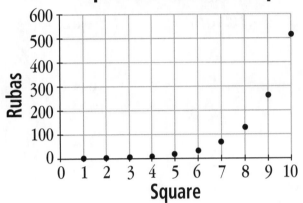

Graph for a Quadratic Relationship

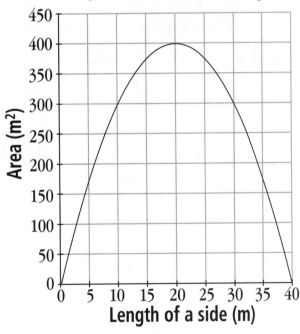

Table for a Linear Relationship

Thickness (layers)	Breaking weight (pennies)
0	0
1	8.4
2	16.8
3	25.2
4	33.6
5	42.0
6	50.4
7	58.8

Table for an Exponential Relationship

Square	Rubas
1	1
2	2
3	4
4	8
5	16
6	32
7	64
8	128
9	256
10	512

Table for a Quadratic Relationship

Length of a side (m)	Area (m^2)
0	0
5	175
10	300
15	375
20	400
25	375
30	300
35	175
40	0

The rectangle below has a perimeter of 20 meters and a side of length l meters.

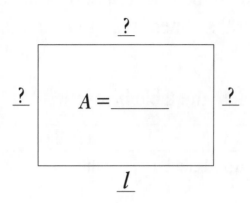

A. Express the length of each side of the rectangle in terms of l. That is, write an expression that contains the variable l to represent the length of each side.

B. Write an equation for the area, A, of the rectangle in terms of l.

C. If the length of a side of the rectangle is 6 meters, what is the area?

D. Use a calculator to make a table and a graph for your equation. Compare your table and graph to those you made in Problem 1.1.

Suppose you own a square piece of land with sides n meters long. You trade your land for a rectangular lot. The length of your new lot is 2 meters longer than the side length of your original lot, and the width of your new lot is 2 meters shorter than the side length of the original lot.

A. Copy and complete the table below.

Original square		New rectangle			Difference
Side length (m)	Area (m²)	Length (m)	Width (m)	Area (m²)	in areas (m²)
3	9	5	1	5	4
4					
5					
6					
7					
n					

B. For each side length in the table, tell how the area of your new lot compares with the area of the original lot. For which side lengths, if any, is this a fair trade?

C. The side length of the original square lot was n meters. For each column in the table, write an expression for the values in the column in terms of n. For example, the expression for the area of the original square is n^2.

A. A square has sides of length x centimeters. A new rectangle is created by increasing one dimension of the square by 2 centimeters.

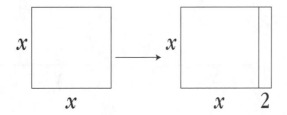

1. The new rectangle is made up of the original square and an added rectangle. What are the dimensions of the added rectangle? What is its area?

2. Write an equation for the area of the new rectangle as the sum of the area of the original square and the area of the added rectangle.

3. What are the length and the width of the new rectangle? Write an equation for the area of the new rectangle as its length times its width.

4. Graph your equations from parts 2 and 3 on your calculator, and copy the graphs onto your paper. Describe the shapes of the graphs. How do the graphs compare? What does this tell you about your two equations?

B. A square has sides of length *x* centimeters. One dimension of the square is increased by 3 centimeters to create a new rectangle.

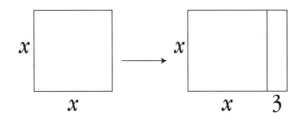

1. How much greater is the area of the new rectangle than the area of the square?

2. Write two equations for the area of the new rectangle.

3. Graph both equations on your calculator, and copy the graphs onto your paper. Describe the shapes of the graphs. How do the graphs compare?

A. A square has sides of length *x* centimeters. A new rectangle is created by increasing one dimension of the square by 2 centimeters and increasing the other dimension by 3 centimeters.

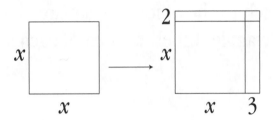

1. Copy the new rectangle. Label the area of each of the four sections.

2. Write two expressions, one in factored form and one in expanded form, for the area of the new rectangle.

3. Use your expressions from part 2 to write two equations for the area, *A*, of the rectangle. Graph both equations on your calculator. Compare these graphs with the graphs you made in Problem 2.2.

B. A square has sides of length x centimeters. One dimension of the square is doubled and then increased by 2 centimeters, and the other dimension is increased by 3 centimeters.

   1. Make a sketch to show how the square is transformed into the new rectangle. Label the area of each section of the new rectangle.

   2. Write two expressions, one in factored form and one in expanded form, for the area of the new rectangle.

   3. Use your expressions from part 2 to write two equations for the area, A, of the rectangle. Graph both equations on your calculator. Compare these graphs with the graphs you made in Problem 2.2.

C. The rectangle below is divided into four smaller rectangles. Write two expressions, one in factored form and one in expanded form, for the area of the large rectangle.

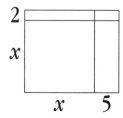

The eight equations below were graphed on a calculator using the window settings shown. Do parts A–F for each equation.

$y = x^2$　　　　　　　$y = x(x + 4)$

$y = x(4 - x)$　　　　$y = (x + 3)(x - 3)$

$y = (x + 3)(x + 3)$　$y = (x + 2)(x + 3)$

$y = x(x - 4)$　　　　$y = 2x(x + 4)$

```
WINDOW
 XMIN=-5
 XMAX=5
 XSCL=1
 YMIN=-10
 YMAX=10
 YSCL=1
```

A. Match the equation to its graph.

B. Label the coordinates of the x-intercepts on the graph. Describe how you can predict the x-intercepts from the equation.

C. Draw the line of symmetry on the graph.

D. Describe the shape of the graph, and label the coordinates of the maximum or minimum point.

E. What features of the graph can you predict from the equation?

F. Draw and label a rectangle whose area is represented by the equation. Then, express the area of the rectangle in expanded form.

Graph 1

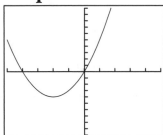

Graph 2

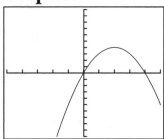

Graph 3

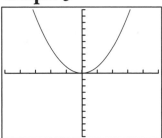

Graph 4

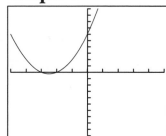

Graph 5

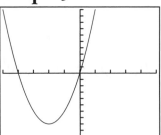

Graph 6

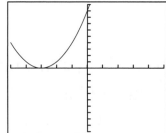

Graph 7

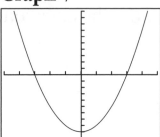

Graph 8

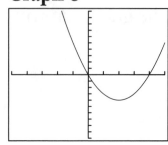

A. Consider case 1, in which two teams have the same number of players. Each player on one team shakes hands with each player on the other team.

   1. How many handshakes will take place between two basketball teams with 10 players each?

   2. How many handshakes will take place between two soccer teams with 15 players each?

   3. Write an equation for the number of handshakes, h, between two teams with n players each.

B. Consider a restricted form of case 2, in which the numbers of players on the two teams differ by 1. Each player on one team shakes hands with each player on the other team.

   1. How many handshakes will take place between a water polo team with 10 players and a water polo team with 9 players?

   2. How many handshakes will take place between a field hockey team with 15 players and a field hockey team with 14 players?

   3. Write an equation for the number of handshakes, h, between a team with n players and a team with $n - 1$ players.

C. Consider case 3, in which each member of a team gives a high five to each teammate.

   1. How many high fives will take place among an academic quiz team with 4 members?

   2. How many high fives will take place among a golf team with 12 members?

   3. Write an equation for the number of high fives, *h*, that will take place among a team with *n* members.

The numbers of dots in the figures below are called **triangular numbers.** The first triangular number is 1, the second is 3, the third is 6, the fourth is 10, and so on.

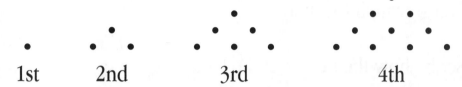

1st   2nd   3rd   4th

A. What two variables are important in this situation? Which is the independent variable, and which is the dependent variable?

B. Look for a pattern in the figures. Use the pattern to help you make a table of the first ten triangular numbers.

Figure number	1	2	3	4	5	6	7	8	9	10
Number of dots (triangular number)										

C. Describe the pattern of change from one triangular number to the next.

D. How can you use this pattern of change to predict the 15th triangular number without making a drawing?

E. Write an equation that can be used to determine the nth triangular number.

F. Does your equation represent a quadratic relationship? Explain.

Suppose you throw a ball straight up into the air. This table describes how the height of the ball might change as it travels through the air.

A. Describe how the height of the ball changes over this 4-second time period.

B. Without making the graph, describe what the graph of these data would look like. Include as many important features as you can.

Time (s)	Height (ft)
0.00	0
0.25	15
0.50	28
0.75	39
1.00	48
1.25	55
1.50	60
1.75	63
2.00	64
2.25	63
2.50	60
2.75	55
3.00	48
3.25	39
3.50	28
3.75	15
4.00	0

C. Do you think these data represent a quadratic function? Explain why or why not.

$$\text{frog:} \quad H = {}^-16t^2 + 12t + 0.2$$
$$\text{flea:} \quad H = {}^-16t^2 + 8t$$
$$\text{basketball player:} \quad H = {}^-16t^2 + 16t + 6.5$$

A. Make tables and graphs of these three equations. Look at heights for time values between 0 seconds and 1 second. In your tables, use intervals of 0.1 second.

Frog	
Time (s)	Height (ft)
0.0	
0.1	
0.2	
0.3	
0.4	
0.5	
0.6	
0.7	
0.8	
0.9	
1.0	

Flea	
Time (s)	Height (ft)
0.0	
0.1	
0.2	
0.3	
0.4	
0.5	
0.6	
0.7	
0.8	
0.9	
1.0	

Basketball Player	
Time (s)	Height (ft)
0.0	
0.1	
0.2	
0.3	
0.4	
0.5	
0.6	
0.7	
0.8	
0.9	
1.0	

$$\begin{aligned}
\text{frog:} \quad & H = {}^-16t^2 + 12t + 0.2 \\
\text{flea:} \quad & H = {}^-16t^2 + 8t \\
\text{basketball player:} \quad & H = {}^-16t^2 + 16t + 6.5
\end{aligned}$$

B. What is the maximum height reached by each jumper, and when is the maximum height reached?

C. How long does each jump last? Explain how you found your answer.

D. What do the constant terms 0.2 and 6.5 tell you about the frog and the basketball player?

Areas of Rectangles with Perimeter 20 Meters

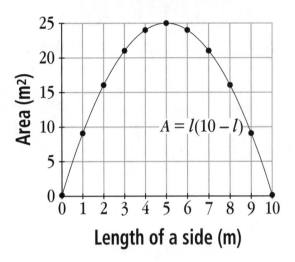

$A = l(10 - l)$

Length of a side (m)

High Fives Exchanged Among the Players on a Team

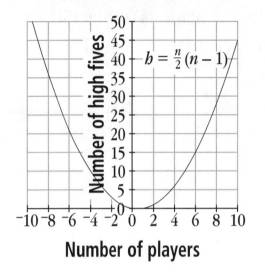

$h = \frac{n}{2}(n - 1)$

Number of players

Square Numbers

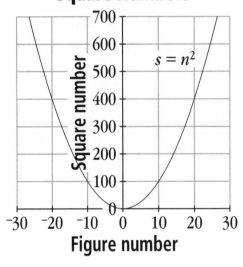

$s = n^2$

Figure number

Height of a Jumping Flea

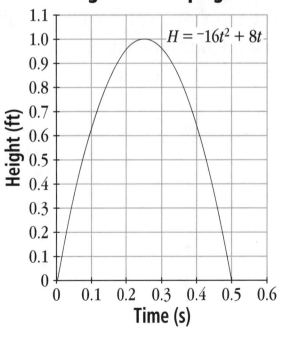

$H = {}^{-}16t^2 + 8t$

Time (s)

For a linear relationship, the y value increases by a constant amount each time the x value increases by 1. In this table for $y = 3x + 1$, the calculations under "First differences" are the differences between consecutive y values. The first differences for $y = 3x + 1$ are all 3.

x	y
0	1
1	4
2	7
3	10
4	13
5	16

First differences

$4 - 1 = 3$

$7 - 4 = 3$

$10 - 7 = 3$

$13 - 10 = 3$

$16 - 13 = 3$

The simplest quadratic relationship is $y = x^2$. The table below shows that the first differences for $y = x^2$ are not constant. However, look at the *second* differences.

x	y
0	0
1	1
2	4
3	9
4	16
5	25

First differences

$1 - 0 = 1$

$4 - 1 = 3$

$9 - 4 = 5$

$16 - 9 = 7$

$25 - 16 = 9$

Second differences

$3 - 1 = 2$

$5 - 3 = 2$

$7 - 5 = 2$

$9 - 7 = 2$

© Prentice-Hall, Inc.

Study the pattern of first and second differences for $y = x^2$.

A. Make a table for each quadratic equation below. Use integer values of x from $^-5$ to 5. Add columns to your tables showing first and second differences.

$y = 2x(x + 3)$ $y = 3x - x^2$

$y = (x - 2)^2$ $y = x^2 + 5x + 6$

B. Consider the patterns of change in the y values and in the first and second differences for the four equations. In what ways are the patterns similar for the four equations? In what ways are they different?

A. 1. A cube with edges of length
2 centimeters is built from centimeter
cubes. If you paint the faces of this cube
and then break it into centimeter cubes,
how many cubes will be painted on three
faces? On two faces? On one face? How
many will be unpainted?

2. Answer the questions from part 1 for cubes with edges of
lengths 3, 4, 5, and 6 centimeters. Organize your data into
a table.

  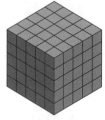 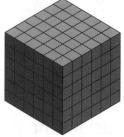

Edge length of large cube	Number of cm cubes	Number of cm cubes painted on			
		3 faces	2 faces	1 face	0 faces
2					
3					
4					
5					
6					

B. Study the patterns in the table. Look for a relationship between the edge length of the large cube and the number of centimeter cubes. Tell whether the pattern of change is linear, quadratic, exponential, or none of these.

C. Look for relationships between the edge length of the large cube and the number of centimeter cubes painted on three faces, two faces, one face, and zero faces. Describe each relationship you find, and tell whether the pattern of change is linear, quadratic, exponential, or none of these.

A large cube with edges of length n centimeters is built from centimeter cubes. The faces of the large cube are painted.

A. Write an equation for the number of centimeter cubes in the large cube.

B. Write an equation for the number of centimeter cubes painted on

    1. three faces   **2.** two faces

    3. one face   **4.** no faces

Dear Family,

The next unit in your child's course of study in mathematics class this year is *Frogs, Fleas, and Painted Cubes.* Your child has already explored a variety of relationships that can be represented with tables, graphs, and equations. This unit focuses on *quadratic* relationships.

Quadratic relationships are encountered in such fields as business, sports, engineering, and economics. We are dealing with quadratic relationships, for example, when we study how the height of a ball—or a jumping flea—changes over time. A quadratic graph, called a *parabola,* is shaped like either a U or an upside-down U.

Students will learn to recognize quadratic patterns of change in tables and graphs, and they will learn to write equations to represent those patterns. They will compare and contrast quadratic patterns of change with those of linear and exponential patterns of change, which they have already studied in depth. Students will again be using graphing calculators to study these relationships. Being able to quickly make a graph of a situation helps students to better understand many of the problems they will encounter.

Here are some strategies for helping your child during this unit:

- Talk with your child about the situations that are presented in the unit.

- Search with your child for other situations that might be modeled by a quadratic equation or graph.

- Review your child's notebook, and ask for explanations of the work.

- Encourage your child's efforts to complete all homework assignments.

As always, if you have any questions or suggestions about your child's mathematics program, please feel free to call.

Sincerely,

Carta a la Familia

Estimada familia,

La próxima unidad del programa de matemáticas de su hijo o hija para este curso se llama *Frogs, Fleas, and Painted Cubes* (Ranas, pulgas y cubos pintados). Su hijo o hija ya ha explorado una variedad de relaciones que pueden representarse mediantes tablas, gráficas y ecuaciones. Esta unidad trata principalmente sobre las relaciones *cuadráticas*.

Las relaciones cuadráticas están presentes en campos como los negocios, los deportes, la ingeniería y la economía. Al estudiar el efecto del tiempo sobre la altura de una pelota o sobre una pulga que va dando saltos, se hace uso de las relaciones cuadráticas. La gráfica cuadrática recibe el nombre de *parábola* y tiene la forma de una U normal o bien la de una U invertida.

Los alumnos aprenderán a identificar en las tablas y en las gráficas patrones cuadráticos de variación y a escribir las ecuaciones que los representen. Además, compararán y contrastarán los patrones cuadráticos de variación con los patrones lineales y exponenciales de variación, los cuales ya fueron ampliamente tratados con anterioridad. Para estudiar dichas relaciones los alumnos volverán a utilizar calculadoras de gráficas, ya que el poder hacer con rapidez la gráfica de una situación determinada les lleva a una mejor comprensión de muchos de los problemas.

Aparecen a continuación algunas estrategias que ustedes pueden emplear para ayudar a su hijo o hija durante el estudio de esta unidad:

- Hablen con él o ella sobre las situaciones presentadas en la unidad.

- Busquen juntos algunas otras situaciones que puedan representarse mediante una ecuación cuadrática o una gráfica.

- Repasen su cuaderno y pídanle que les explique su trabajo.

- Anímenle a esforzarse para que complete toda la tarea.

Y como de costumbre, si ustedes tienen alguna duda o recomendación relacionada con el programa de matemáticas de su hijo o hija, no duden en llamarnos.

Atentamente,

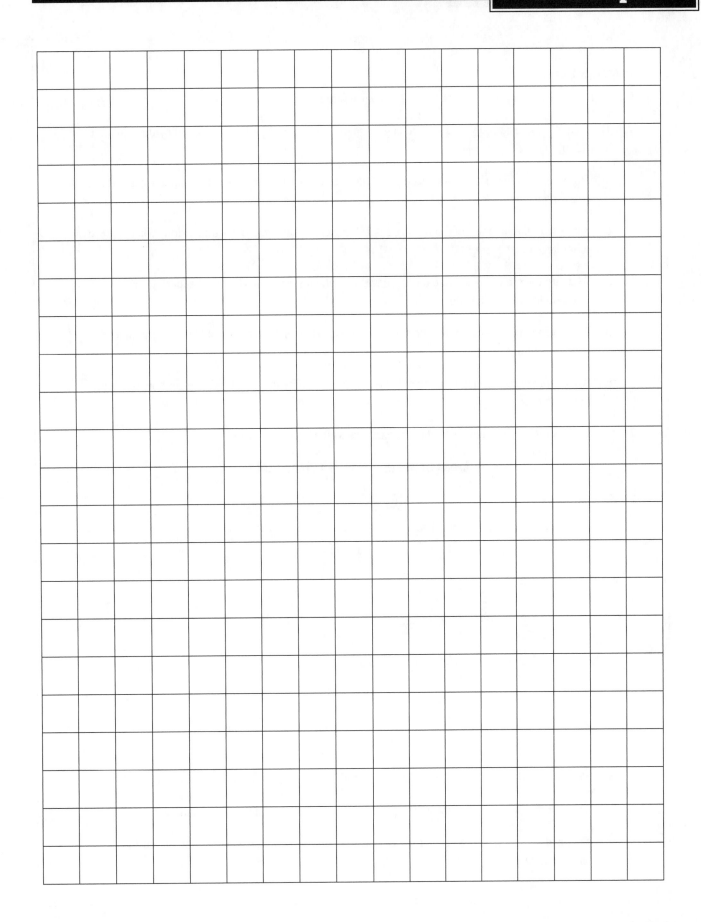

Investigation 1

Use these problems for additional practice after Investigation 1.

1. The area, A, of a rectangle with a side of length l meters and a fixed perimeter is given by the equation $A = l(240 - l)$.

    a. Suppose one dimension of the rectangle is 180 meters. What is the other dimension? What is the area of the rectangle?

    b. Suppose one dimension of the rectangle is 110 meters. What is the other dimension? What is the area of the rectangle?

    c. What are the dimensions of the rectangle with the greatest area possible for this perimeter? Explain how you found your answer.

    d. What are the dimensions of the rectangle with this perimeter and an area of 8000 square meters? Explain your answer.

    e. What is the fixed perimeter for the rectangles represented by this equation? Explain how you found the perimeter.

2. The graph shows length and area data for rectangles with a fixed perimeter.

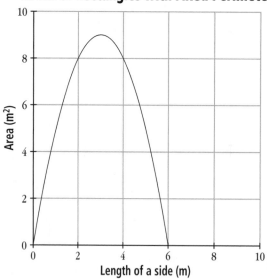

Areas of Rectangles with Fixed Perimeter

    a. What are the dimensions of the rectangle with this perimeter and an area of 8 square meters?

    b. What are the dimensions of the rectangle with this perimeter and an area of 5 square meters?

    c. What is the greatest area possible for a rectangle with this perimeter? What are the dimensions of this rectangle?

   d. What are the greatest and the least side lengths possible for a rectangle with this perimeter? What area corresponds with these side lengths?

   e. What is the fixed perimeter for the rectangles represented by the graph? Explain how you found the perimeter.

3. A family of rectangles has a fixed perimeter of 56 square inches.

   a. Write an equation for the area, A, in terms of the length of a side, l.

   b. Copy the table below. Use your equation to fill in the missing values.

Length of a side (in)	Area (in²)
0	
7	
	196
28	
21	
	180

   c. Use your equation and your table to help you sketch a graph of the relationship between the length of a side and the area.

   d. What are the dimensions of the rectangle with the greatest area for this perimeter?

Investigation 2

Use these problems for additional practice after Investigation 2.

1. Refer to the diagram below to answer parts a–f.

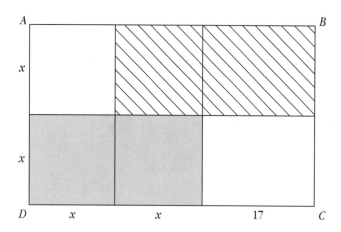

   a. Write an expression for the area of the diagonally shaded region.

   b. Write an expression for the area of the gray region.

   c. Write an expression for the total area of the white regions.

   d. Write an expression for the difference in area between the diagonally shaded region and the gray region.

   e. Write an expression for the perimeter of rectangle *ABCD*.

   f. Write an expression for the area of rectangle *ABCD*.

2. A square has a perimeter of 8*x* centimeters.

   a. Draw a square whose perimeter is represented by the expression 8*x*. Label the length of each side.

   b. Write an expression for the area of the square.

   c. Suppose the perimeter of the square is 24 centimeters. What is the side length of the square? What is the area of the square?

   d. If the side length of the square with perimeter 8*x* were doubled, what would the new side length be?

   e. If the side length of the square with perimeter 8*x* were doubled, what would the new area be?

In 3–5, draw and label a rectangle whose area is represented by the expression. Then write an equivalent expression in expanded form.

3. $(x + 1)(x + 5)$ **4.** $3x(x - 4)$ **5.** $(x + 6)(x + 2)$

In 6–11, write the expression in factored form. You may want to draw a rectangle to illustrate the area represented by the expression.

6. $x^2 + 2x + 9x + 18$ **7.** $x^2 + 4x$ **8.** $x^2 + 12x + 36$

9. $x^2 + 2x + 7x + 14$ **10.** $x^2 + 7x + 12$ **11.** $x^2 + 12x + 27$

12. Serena and Chuck had a large square piece of cardboard for designing a poster advertising the upcoming drama club fund-raiser. They decided to trim 3 feet from the length of the cardboard.

3 ft

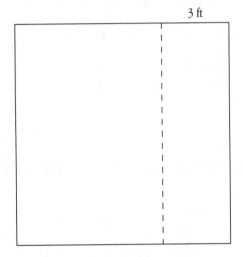

Suppose each side of the original square of cardboard had a length of x feet.

a. Write an expression for the area of the strip that Serena and Chuck trimmed from the large piece.

b. Write an expression for the area of the remaining piece of cardboard.

c. Write an expression for the perimeter of the strip that Serena and Chuck trimmed from the large piece.

d. Write an expression for the perimeter of the remaining piece of cardboard.

e. The perimeter of the original piece of cardboard was 36 feet.

    i. What is the area of the strip that Serena and Chuck trimmed from the large piece?

    ii. What is the area of the remaining piece of cardboard?

    iii. What is the perimeter of the remaining piece of cardboard?

Investigation 3

Use these problems for additional practice after Investigation 3.

1. The pattern below represents a sequence of numbers as collections of squares.

  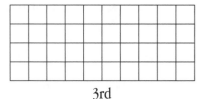

1st   2nd   3rd

   a. What are the next two numbers to be represented in the sequence?

   b. Describe the pattern of change from one rectangular pattern to the next.

   c. Use the pattern of change you have described to predict the 6th and 7th numbers in the sequence.

   d. Which equation below can be used to find the nth number in the sequence, where c is the nth number? Test the equation by seeing whether it produces the sequence of numbers shown in the rectangular patterns.

   $$c = (n + 1)(n + 3) \qquad c = (n + 1)(3n + 1) \qquad c = n + 1(3n + 1)$$

2. The unshaded squares in the grids below represent a sequence of numbers. The first three numbers in the sequence are 99, 96, and 91.

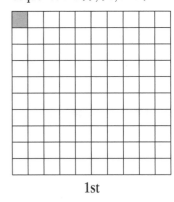 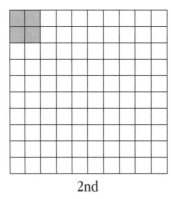 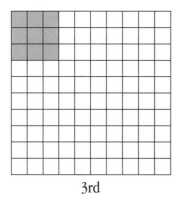

1st   2nd   3rd

   a. What are the next two numbers to be represented in the sequence?

   b. Describe the pattern of change from one grid to the next.

   c. Use the pattern of change you have described to predict the 6th and 7th numbers in the sequence.

   d. Write an equation for calculating the nth number in the sequence. Test your equation by seeing whether it produces the sequence of numbers shown in the grids.

    e. This sequence of the numbers is an example of a *finite sequence*, which means that the sequence does not go on forever but eventually comes to an end. How many numbers are in the sequence? Explain your reasoning.

3. The number sequence 2, 6, 12, 20, 30, . . . , follows a pattern.

    a. Describe the pattern of change between the numbers in the sequence.

    b. Use the pattern you have described to predict the next three numbers in the sequence.

    c. Sketch a pattern of rectangles to represent this sequence. The area of each rectangle should represent its number in the sequence.

    d. Write an equation for calculating the nth number in the sequence. Test your equation by seeing whether it produces the sequence of numbers shown in the rectangular patterns you sketched in part c.

    e. Is 117 in the sequence? If it is in the sequence, explain which number in the sequence it is. If it is not in the sequence, explain why not.

    f. Is 10,100 in the sequence? If it is in the sequence, explain which number in the sequence it is. If it is not in the sequence, explain why not.

Investigation 4

Use these problems for additional practice after Investigation 4.

1. A ship conducting oceanographic research drops anchor offshore Honiara, the capitol of the Solomon Islands in the South Pacific. When the anchor is tossed into the water, the depth in feet, D, it descends in t seconds is given by the equation $D = -4t^2 + 12t$.

   a. If it takes the anchor 10 seconds to reach the bottom, how deep is the water where the ship has dropped anchor?

   b. If the ship moves to another location and the anchor takes 8.5 seconds to reach the bottom, how deep is the water in that spot?

   c. If the ship anchors in the harbor of Honiara, where the water is 72 feet deep (that is, $D = -72$), how long will it take for the anchor to reach the bottom when it is dropped?

2. Metropolitan Container produces storage containers from recycled plastic. The total cost in dollars, C, of manufacturing n containers is given by the equation $C = 2n^2 + 9n + 100$.

   a. What is the total cost of manufacturing 4 containers?

   b. What is the total cost of manufacturing 10 containers?

   c. The *average cost* of manufacturing each container is $\frac{C}{n}$, or the total cost of manufacturing the containers divided by the number of containers.

      i. Based on your answer to part a, what is the average cost of manufacturing 4 containers?

      ii. Based on your answer to part b, what is the average cost of manufacturing 10 containers?

      iii. Compare your answers to parts i and ii. What can you say about manufacturing 4 containers versus 10 containers?

   d. The city of Metropolis has placed an order with Metropolitan Container for a certain number of containers. If the cost of producing the containers the city has ordered is $3660, how many containers did the city order? Explain how you found your answer.

In 3 and 4, do parts a–d.

3. $y = x^2 - 4$ 4. $y = 9 - x^2$

   a. Sketch a graph of the equation.

   b. Find the coordinates of the points where the graph crosses the x- and y-axes, and label these points on your graph.

   c. Find the coordinates of the minimum or maximum point, and label this point on your graph.

   d. Label the line of symmetry.

5. Use the graph below to answer parts a–f.

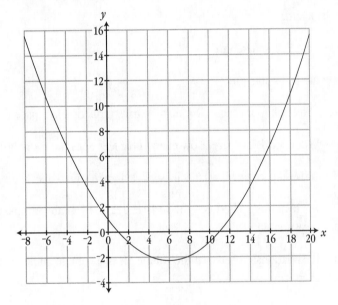

   a. What are the coordinates of the minimum point of the parabola?

   b. At what point does the line of symmetry cross the x- or y-axis?

   c. What are the coordinates of the points where the graph crosses the x-axis?

   d. What are the coordinates of the point where the graph crosses the y-axis?

   e. Could $y = 3 - x^2$ be the equation of this graph? Explain why or why not.

   f. Could $y = x^2 - 12x + 100$ be the equation of this graph? Explain why or why not.

Investigation 5

Use these problems for additional practice after Investigation 5.

In 1–8, refer to the diagrams below, which illustrate relationships among units for measuring distance, area, and volume.

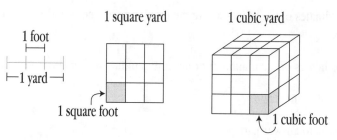

1. How many feet are in 1 yard?

2. How many square feet are in 1 square yard?

3. How many cubic feet are in 1 cubic yard?

4. A house has 936 square feet of floor space. How many square yards of floor space does the house have?

5. A storage room has 45 cubic yards of space. How many cubic feet does the room hold?

6. If a cube measures 2 yards on each edge, what is its surface area in square feet?

7. Write an equation for the relationship between the surface area, S, of a cube in square feet and the edge length, e, of the cube measured in yards.

8. Write an equation for the relationship between the volume, V, of a cube in cubic yards and the edge length, e, of the cube measured in feet.

In 9–12, explain your reasoning. Draw diagrams if they are helpful to you.

9. The surface area of a cube is 294 square centimeters. What is the edge length of the cube?

10. The volume of a cube is 1331 cubic meters. What is the edge length of the cube?

11. A large cube is made by gluing centimeter cubes together. Each layer of the cube is made from 36 centimeter cubes.

    a. What is the edge length of the large cube?

    b. What is the surface area of the large cube?

    c. What is the volume of the large cube?

12. The volume of a cube is 125 cubic centimeters. What is the surface area of the cube?

Blackline Masters and Additional Practice for *Say It with Symbols*

Labsheet

Transparencies

Additional Resources

Additional Practice

Problem 3.3 Trapezoids

The marketing manager wants to make a table showing admission prices for groups with certain numbers of adults and children.

Group Admission Prices

		Number of children			
	20	40	60	80	100
Number of adults — 10					
20					
30					
40					

A. Copy and complete the table. Do your calculations without using a calculator.

B. Look for patterns in the rows and columns. Describe each pattern you find, and tell which part of the equation creates the pattern.

C. In the equation $p = 100 + 10a + 8c$, what do the numbers 100, 10, and 8 tell you about calculating the group price?

D. What mathematical operations do you need to perform to calculate the group price for a particular number of adults and children? In what order must you perform the operations?

The daily concession profit can be predicted by the equation $P = 2.50V - 500$. This profit equation was used to derive the following equation for the *average* daily concession profit per visitor:

$$A = \frac{2.50V - 500}{V}$$

A. 1. If 300 people visit the park, about how much concession profit will be made?

   2. About how much concession profit will be made per visitor?

B. Copy and complete the table below to show the average per-visitor concession profit for various numbers of visitors. Do your calculations without using a calculator.

Visitors	100	200	300	400	500	600	700	800
Average profit								

C. Find the average per-visitor concession profit for 250, 350, and 425 visitors.

D. What mathematical operations do you need to perform to calculate the average per-visitor profit for a given number of visitors?

In what order must you perform the operations?

E. The Water Works business manager claims that the average concession profit per visitor can also be calculated with either of these equations:

$$A = \tfrac{1}{V}(2.50V - 500)$$

$$A = (2.50V - 500) \div V$$

Do you agree? Explain.

The equation below gives the height, y, of the arch above a point x feet from one of the bases of the arch. If you are standing under the arch x feet from one base, the point of the arch directly over your head will be $25x - 0.5x^2$ feet above the ground.

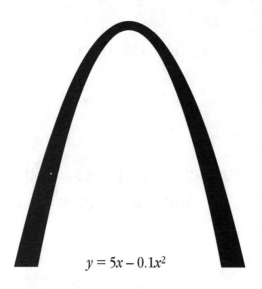

$$y = 5x - 0.1x^2$$

A. Use the equation to find the height of the arch at these distances from the left base. Do your calculations without using a calculator.

1. 10 feet

2. 30 feet

3. 50 feet

© Prentice-Hall, Inc.

B. What operations did you perform to calculate your answers for part A? In what order did you perform these operations?

C. Check your answers for part A by using a graphing calculator to help you make a table.

D. 1. The expression $5x - 0.1x^2$ is equivalent to the expression $0.1x(50 - x)$. Use this second expression to calculate the heights for the x values given in part A.

   2. In what order did you perform the operations?

If a square pool has sides of length *s* feet, how many tiles are needed to form the border?

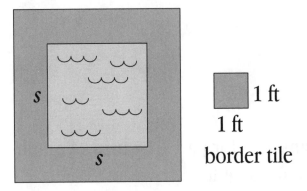

A. Make sketches on grid paper to help you figure out how many tiles are needed for borders of square pools with sides of length 1, 2, 3, 4, 6, and 10 feet. Record your results in a table.

B. Write an equation for the number of tiles, *N*, needed to form a border for a square pool with sides of length *s* feet.

C. Try to write at least one more equation for the number of tiles needed for the border of the pool. How could you convince someone that your expressions are equivalent?

Takashi thought of the pool's border as being composed of four 1-by-s rectangles, each made from s tiles, and four corner squares, each made from one tile. He wrote the expression $4s + 4$ to represent the total number of border tiles.

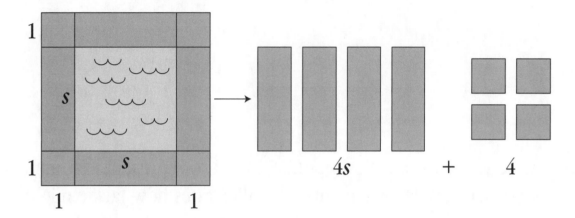

A. Stella wrote the expression $4(s + 1)$ to represent the number of border tiles. Draw a picture that illustrates how Stella might have been thinking about the border of the pool.

B. Jeri wrote the expression $s + s + s + s + 4$ to represent the number of border tiles. Draw a picture that illustrates how Jeri might have been thinking about the border of the pool.

C. Sal wrote the expression $2s + 2(s + 2)$ to represent the number of border tiles. Draw a picture that illustrates how Sal might have been thinking about the border of the pool.

D. Jackie wrote the expression $4(s + 2) - 4$ to represent the number of border tiles. Draw a picture that illustrates how Jackie might have been thinking about the border of the pool.

E. Explain why each expression in parts A–D is equivalent to Takashi's expression.

Below are four designs for pools with swimming and diving sections. For each design, show two methods for calculating the total surface area of the water. Then tell which method is more efficient. That is, tell which method requires fewer mathematical operations.

A.

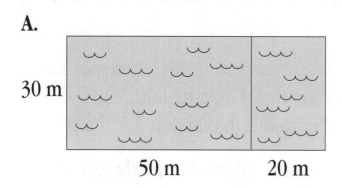

30 m

50 m   20 m

B.

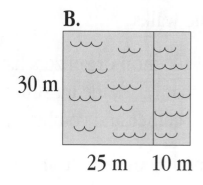

30 m

25 m   10 m

C.

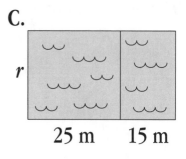

r

25 m   15 m

D.

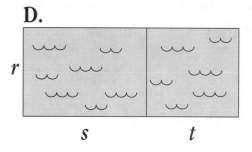

r

s   t

Leanne, Gilberto, and Alana are participating in a walkathon.

- Leanne asks her sponsors to pledge $1 for each mile she walks.
- Gilberto asks his sponsors to pledge $2 for each mile he walks.
- Alana asks her sponsors to pledge $5 plus $0.50 for each mile she walks.

The walkathon organizers have offered a prize to the three-person team that raises the most money. Leanne, Gilberto, and Alana will walk together and combine their earnings to compete for the prize.

Leanne has pledges from 16 sponsors, Gilberto has pledges from 7 sponsors, and Alana has pledges from 11 sponsors.

A. For each student, write an equation for the amount of money the student will raise if he or she walks x miles. Then write an equation for the total amount the three-person team will raise if they walk x miles.

$A_{\text{Leanne}} =$

$A_{\text{Gilberto}} =$

$A_{\text{Alana}} =$

$A_{\text{total}} =$

B. Alana asked each of her 11 sponsors to pledge $5 in addition to an amount per mile, so the team will raise $55 regardless of how far they walk.

    1. Excluding the $55, how much will the team raise per mile?

    2. Use your answer from part 1 to help you write a different equation for the total amount the team will raise if they walk x miles.

C. **1.** Use the distributive and commutative properties to show that the two expressions you wrote for the total amount the team will raise are equivalent.

    2. Verify that the expressions are equivalent by making and comparing tables or graphs.

At their planning meeting, the organizers of the hospital walkathon discussed expenses and income. They made the following estimates:

- Expense for posters and newspaper, radio, and TV ads: $500

- Expense for souvenir T-shirts for participants: $6 per child, $8.50 per adult

- Income from business sponsors whose logos will appear on T-shirts and signs: $1000

- Expense for paramedics and an ambulance in case of emergency: $250

- Income from registration fees: $5 per child, $15 per adult

Notice that some of the expenses are fixed, while others depend on the number of adults and children who participate.

The difference between the total income and the total expenses is the profit. The organizers will donate any profit from the event to the hospital.

© Prentice-Hall, Inc.

A. Estimate the total income, the total expenses, and the total profit if 40 children and 30 adults participate in the walkathon.

B. Write two equivalent expressions for the total income in terms of the number of adults, a, and the number of children, c, who participate.

C. Write two equivalent expressions for the total expenses in terms of the number of adults, a, and the number of children, c, who participate.

D. Use parentheses and your results from parts B and C to write an expression showing the profit as total income minus total expenses. That is, express the profit as (expression for income) − (expression for expenses).

E. Write an expression for profit that is equivalent to your expression from part D but that is as short as possible. Use the distributive and commutative properties to show that the two profit expressions are equivalent.

F. Evaluate your profit expressions from parts D and E for $a = 100$ and $c = 75$. Can you conclude from your results that the expressions are equivalent? Explain.

G. Compare the profit expressions you wrote in parts D and E. What are the advantages and disadvantages of writing the profit expression in a shorter form?

Tua, Sam, and Carlos made the drawings below to illustrate their methods for calculating the area of a trapezoid. Try to figure out how each student thought about the problem.

Tua's method

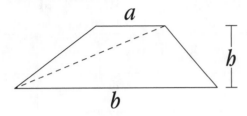

Sam's method

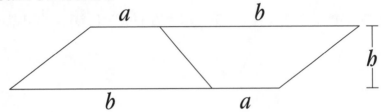

Carlos's method

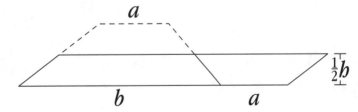

A. Explain each student's method for finding the area.

B. Write an algebraic expression to describe each method.

C. Show that the expressions you wrote in part B are equivalent.

In parts A–C, you will explore three ways of thinking about this question: If a league has n teams and each team plays each of the other teams twice, how many games are played in all?

A. Figure out how many games would be played for leagues with 2, 3, 4, 5, and 6 teams. Record your results in a table.

Number of teams	2	3	4	5	6
Number of games					

Look for a pattern in your table. Use the pattern to write an expression for the number of games played by a league with n teams.

B. Suppose a sports reporter wants to attend exactly one game in the schedule of an n-team league.

1. How many choices does the reporter have for the home team for the game she attends?

2. Once she has chosen a home team, how many choices does she have for the visiting team?

3. Use your answers from parts 1 and 2 to write an expression for the total number of games the reporter can choose from.

© Prentice-Hall, Inc.

C. Suppose you made a table to record wins and losses for an *n*-team league.

Visiting Team

	T_1	T_2	T_3	$\cdots$	T_n
T_1					
T_2					
T_3					
$\vdots$					
T_n					

Home Team

1. How many cells would your table have?

2. How many cells in the table would not be used for *W* or *L* entries?

3. Use your answers from parts 1 and 2 to write an expression for the total number of games played.

D. In parts A–C, you wrote expressions for the number of games played by an *n*-team league. Show that these expressions are equivalent.

bid 1: cost = $100 + $4 × the number of books printed
bid 2: cost = $25 + $7 × the number of books printed

If you let x represent the number of books printed and y represent the cost in dollars, the equations become $y = 100 + 4x$ and $y = 25 + 7x$.

Use your graphing calculator to help answer parts A–C.

A. Make a table of x and y values for each bid. Use your table to find the number of books for which the two bids are equal. Explain your work.

B. Make a graph of the two equations. Use your graph to find the number of books for which the two bids are equal. Copy the graph onto your paper, and use it to help explain how you found your answer.

C. For what numbers of books is bid 1 less than bid 2? Explain how you found your answer.

You can solve many equations by operating on the symbols. In Problem 4.1, the equation for bid 1 is $y = 100 + 4x$, where y is the cost and x is the number of books printed.

To find out how many books can be printed for $300, you can solve the equation $300 = 100 + 4x$ for the variable x.

In your earlier mathematics work, you learned that to solve linear equations such as $300 = 100 + 4x$, you need to *undo* the mathematical operations until x is alone on one side of the equation.

To make sure the sides of the equation remain equal, you must apply any mathematical operation to *both* sides. This *symbolic method* of solution is illustrated below.

$$300 = 100 + 4x$$

$$300 - 100 = 100 - 100 + 4x$$

Since 100 is added to $4x$, subtract 100 from *both sides* of the equation.

$$200 = 4x$$

$$\frac{200}{4} = \frac{4x}{4}$$

Since x is multiplied by 4, divide *both sides* by 4.

$$50 = x$$

Now x is alone on one side of the equation. It is easy to see that the solution is 50. This means that 50 books can be printed for $300.

The example below shows one way to solve the equation $100 + 4x = 25 + 7x$.

$$100 + 4x = 25 + 7x$$
$$100 + 4x - 4x = 25 + 7x - 4x \qquad 1.$$
$$100 = 25 + 3x$$
$$100 - 25 = 25 + 3x - 25 \qquad 2.$$
$$75 = 3x$$
$$\frac{75}{3} = \frac{3x}{3} \qquad 3.$$
$$25 = x$$

A. Supply an explanation for each numbered step in the above solution to $100 + 4x = 25 + 7x$.

B. The solution above begins by subtracting $4x$ from both sides of the equation. Show a solution that begins with a different step.

C. How can you check that $x = 25$ is the correct solution? Show that your method works.

In A–D, use the symbolic method to solve the equation.

A. $7x + 15 = 12x + 5$

B. $14 - 3x = 1.5x + 5$

C. $-3x + 5 = 2x - 10$

D. $3 + 5(x + 2) = 7x - 1$

E. Check your solutions to the equations in A–D.

F. Look over your work for A–D. Record any general strategies that seem to work well in solving linear equations.

Finding the x-intercepts of the graph of $y = x^2 + 5x$ is the same as solving the equation $x^2 + 5x = 0$.

In earlier units, you solved quadratic equations by using tables and graphs. For example, to solve $x^2 + 5x = 0$, you can trace a graph of $y = x^2 + 5x$ to find x values for which $y = 0$. Or you can make a table of values and look for the x values that correspond to a y value of 0.

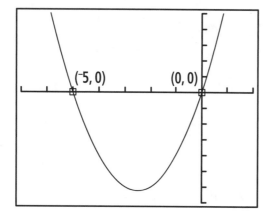

x	y
-7	14
-6	6
-5	**0**
-4	-4
-3	-6
-2	-6
-1	-4
0	**0**
1	6
2	14
3	24

The solutions to $x^2 + 5x = 0$ are called the **roots** of the equation $y = x^2 + 5x$. A quadratic equation may have zero, one, or two roots. If r is a root of an equation, then the point $(r, 0)$ is an x-intercept of the graph.

A. The expression $x^2 + 3x$ is in expanded form. Write an equivalent expression in factored form.

B. Find all possible solutions to the equation $x^2 + 3x = 0$. Explain how you know you have found all the solutions.

C. What are the x-intercepts of $y = x^2 + 3x$? Explain how your answers to part B can help you answer this question.

D. Which form of the expression $x^2 + 3x$, the expanded form or the factored form, is more useful for finding the roots, or x-intercepts, of the equation $y = x^2 + 3x$? Explain your reasoning.

E. In 1 and 2, an equation is given for both the factored form and the expanded form of a quadratic expression. Find the roots, or *x*-intercepts, of the equation without making a table or a graph, and tell which form of the equation you used to find your answer.

1. $y = 4x^2 - 8x$ or $y = 4x(x - 2)$

2. $y = 6x(5 - 2x)$ or $y = 30x - 12x^2$

F. In 1–3, solve the equation by first factoring the quadratic expression.

1. $x^2 + 4.5x = 0$

2. $x^2 - 9x = 0$

3. $-x^2 + 10x = 0$

You will need four to six rods of the same length and several unit rods. In this problem, you will find the surface area of stacks of the longer rods. The rods in each stack should be staggered by 1 unit, as shown below.

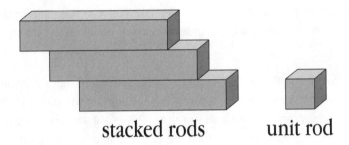

stacked rods   unit rod

A. Use the unit rods to determine the dimensions of one of the longer rods.

B. Find the surface area of a single rod, a stack of two rods, a stack of three rods, and so on.

C. Use your findings to help you write an equation for the relationship between the surface area, A, and the number of rods in the stack, N.

Dear Family,

The next unit that your child will be studying in mathematics class this year explores the topic that beginning algebra used to focus on almost exclusively: the use of symbols. When you first began studying algebra, you probably spent most of your time learning to manipulate symbols. Chances are you didn't get a chance to think about what the symbols actually meant in terms of the real world. This mathematics curriculum emphasizes the *meaning* behind the symbols. This helps students to build their own understanding of the basics of algebra and its usefulness for solving everyday problems.

Say It with Symbols focuses on the distributive property, which demonstrates a relationship between multiplication and addition. A good understanding of this relationship will take your child a long way in making sense of algebraic symbols. Students will also be reviewing what they have learned about linear and quadratic relationships and the connections among graphs, tables, and verbal statements. Often, students will find more than one way to represent a solution symbolically. This gives them a reason for developing ways to show that some algebraic expressions that look different are actually the same.

Here are some strategies for helping your child during this unit:

- Talk with your child about the situations that are presented and why we can rearrange symbols as shown in the unit.

- Ask your child to show you a problem that can be represented by more than one algebraic expression. Have your child demonstrate that the expressions are actually the same and what they mean in terms of the problem.

- Talk with your child about the importance of being skillful in algebra.

- Encourage your child's efforts in completing all homework assignments.

As always, if you have any questions or suggestions about your child's mathematics program, please feel free to call.

Sincerely,

Estimada familia,

La próxima unidad que su hijo o hija estudiará este año en la clase de matemáticas trata sobre lo que anteriormente fue el tema principal y casi exclusivo en los procesos de iniciación al álgebra: el uso de los símbolos. Cuando antes se comenzaba a estudiar álgebra por primera vez, lo normal era pasar la mayoría del tiempo aprendiendo a manejar los símbolos. Y lo más probable era que no se presentara ninguna oportunidad para pensar en lo que realmente significaban los mismos con relación al mundo real. En cambio, en este programa de matemáticas se destaca la importancia del significado de los símbolos. Esto ayudará a los alumnos a aumentar tanto sus propios conocimientos sobre las nociones básicas del álgebra como sobre la utilidad de ésta para resolver problemas de la vida diaria.

Say It with Symbols (Díselo con Símbolos) trata principalmente sobre la propiedad distributiva, la cual demuestra una relación entre la multiplicación y la adición. Su hijo o hija, cuando llegue a entender bien dicha relación, habrá dado un paso decisivo hacia la comprensión de los símbolos algebraicos. Además de esto, los alumnos repasarán lo aprendido sobre las relaciones lineales y cuadráticas y sobre las conexiones existentes entre gráficas, tablas y enunciados verbales. Es frecuente que consigan encontrar más de una manera de representar una solución mediante símbolos. Así tendrán un motivo para desarrollar caminos alternativos que muestren que algunas expresiones algebraicas aparentemente diferentes son en realidad iguales.

He aquí algunas estrategias que ustedes pueden emplear para ayudar a su hijo o hija en esta unidad:

- Comenten con él o ella las situaciones presentadas y las razones por las que los símbolos pueden colocarse de distintas formas, como puede verse en la unidad.

- Pídanle que les muestre un problema que pueda representarse por más de una expresión algebraica. Díganle que demuestre que en realidad dichas expresiones son iguales y cuál es su significado con relación al problema.

- Comenten juntos la importancia de dominar las técnicas del álgebra.

- Anímenle a esforzarse para que complete toda la tarea.

Y como de costumbre, si ustedes tienen alguna duda o recomendación relacionada con el programa de matemáticas de su hijo o hija, no duden en llamarnos.

Atentamente,

Grid Paper

Investigation 1

Use these problems for additional practice after Investigation 1.

In 1–26, evaluate the expression for the given value of x.

1. $3.5x - 10$ when $x = 2$

2. $45 - 2x$ when $x = 6$

3. $-3 - x$ when $x = \frac{1}{2}$

4. $4x + 9$ when $x = 11$

5. $2x^2$ when $x = 8$

6. $11 - 3x^2$ when $x = 1$

7. $4.5 + x^2$ when $x = 1.5$

8. $6x^2 + 13$ when $x = -10$

9. $6x^2 + x - 11$ when $x = 2$

10. $6x^2 + x - 11$ when $x = -2$

11. $12 - 2x^2 + 5x$ when $x = -4$

12. $12 - 2x^2 + 5x$ when $x = 4$

13. $x(31 - x)$ when $x = 3$

14. $(x + 5)(x - 1)$ when $x = 0$

15. $(x - 1.5)(x + 42)$ when $x = 1.5$

16. $(31 - x)x$ when $x = -3$

17. $\frac{36}{x^2}$ when $x = -6$

18. $\frac{x^2}{24}(x + 7)$ when $x = -7$

19. $42(x + 1)$ when $x = 4$

20. $\frac{3(16 - x)}{2x}$ when $x = 10$

21. $\frac{x}{4} + 6(x - 12)$ when $x = 12$

22. $7x(3 + x)$ when $x = -4$

23. $7x^2 - x + 10$ when $x = 2$

24. $8x - 2x(6 - x)$ when $x = 0$

25. $0.5x^2 + x - 20$ when $x = 10$

26. $(x + 7)(x - 2)$ when $x = -5$

27. When Michael and his three friends go to the movies, they each either skate to the theater or ride a bike. The number of wheels in the group as they go to the theater is given by the equation $W = 8s + 2b$, where s is the number of friends skating and b is the number of friends biking.

    a. If Michael decides to skate and his friends decide to bike, how many wheels are in the group?

    b. If everyone decides to skate, how many wheels are in the group?

    c. In the equation $W = 8s + 2b$, explain why the variable s has a coefficient of 8 and the variable b has a coefficient of 2.

    d. Suppose that as Michael and his three friends go to the movies, there are 26 wheels in the group. How many are on skates and how many are riding a bike? Explain how you found your answer.

28. A car is stopped at a red light. When the light turns green, the car begins moving forward. The distance in feet of the car from the light after t seconds is given by the equation $D = 4t^2$.

   a. How far is the car from the light after 5 seconds?

   b. How far is the car from the light after 10 seconds?

   c. How far is the car from the light at $t = 0$ seconds? Explain why your answer makes sense.

29. Susan has a piggy bank into which she puts only nickels. The amount of money in dollars, D, in the bank is given by $D = \frac{n}{20}$, where n is the number of nickels in the piggy bank.

   a. If Susan has 80 nickels in her piggy bank, how many dollars does she have?

   b. If Susan has 94 nickels in her piggy bank, how many dollars does she have?

   c. Based on your answers to parts a and b, explain why the equation makes sense.

Investigation 2

Use these problems for additional practice after Investigation 2.

1. A cube has an edge length of *r*.

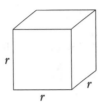

 a. What is the sum of the lengths of all the edges of the cube if $r = 4$?

 b. Write two equations for the sum, *S*, of the lengths of all the edges of a cube with edge length *r*.

2. A rectangular box has length *L*, width *W*, and height *H*.

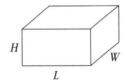

 a. What is the sum of the lengths of all the edges of the box if $L = 3$, $W = 2$, and $H = 1.5$? Show how you found your answer.

 b. Write two equations for the sum, *S*, of the lengths of all the edges of a box with length *L*, width *W*, and height *H*.

The rectangle below has length *L* and width *W*. Use the diagram to answer 3–6.

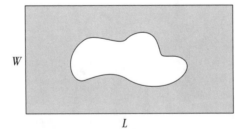

3. Write two equations for the perimeter, *P*, of the rectangle.

4. Suppose the length of the rectangle is equal to twice the width, or 2*W*.

 a. If the width of the rectangle is 1.5, what is the length?

 b. If the width is 2, what is the perimeter?

 c. Write two equations for the perimeter of the rectangle, *P*, in terms of only the width, *W*.

5. If $L = 14$ meters and $W = 6.5$ meters, what is the area of the shaded region inside the rectangle if the area of the blob is 38 square meters? Show how you found your answer.

6. Write an equation for the area, A, of the shaded region inside the rectangle if the area of the blob is Q.

Investigation 3

Use these problems for additional practice after Investigation 3.

1. **a.** Write 45 as a product of two factors.

    b. Write 45 as a product of three factors.

    c. Write 45 as a product of two factors, such that one factor is the sum of two terms.

    d. Write $45x$ as a product of two factors.

    e. Write $45x$ as the sum of three terms.

    f. Write $45x$ as a product of two factors, such that one factor is the sum of two terms, in at least two ways.

In 2–5, rewrite the statement with a number or an expression in each blank to make the statement true.

2. $\_\_ (6 + \_\_ x) = 6x + 18$

3. $\_\_ (8 - 2) = \_\_ x$

4. $3x(3 + \_\_) = 10x$

5. $11(\_\_ + 3 \_\_) = 33x - 11$

In 6–9, write two expressions that are equivalent to the given expression.

6. $7(x - 4)$

7. $x(5 - 6) + 13x - 10$

8. $2.5(8 - 2x) + 5(x + 1)$

9. $3(x + 10) - 3(2 - 4x)$

In 10–17, write the quadratic equation in factored form.

10. $y = 3x + 21x^2$

11. $q = 72r^2 - 24r$

12. $y = 5x^2 + 10x$

13. $a = 16b - 48b^2$

14. $y = 3(x - 1) + (x - 1)$

15. $y = x^2 + 3x + 2$

16. $y = x(x - 10) + x(2x + 5)$

17. $y = 52x^2 - 13$

18. The Metropolis Middle School volleyball team is operating the concession stand at school basketball games to help raise money for new uniforms. The profit in dollars, P, from operating the stand is given by the equation $P = N - 0.5(\frac{N}{5} + 300)$, where N is the total number of items sold.

    a. How much money will the volleyball team raise if they sell 400 items?

    b. How much money will the volleyball team raise if they sell 550 items?

    c. If the team needs to raise $1000 for new uniforms, will they have to sell more than or fewer than 1000 items? Explain your reasoning.

    d. Write another equation for P.

19. Each side of the figure has length *X*.

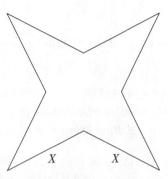

a. If $X = 3.5$, what is the perimeter of the figure?

b. If $X = 10$, what is the perimeter of the figure?

c. Write three equations for the perimeter, *P*, of the figure.

d. Show that your three expressions for the perimeter are equivalent.

20. Refer to the figure below to answer a–d.

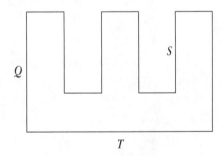

a. If $Q = 4$ m, $S = 3$ m, and $T = 7$ m, what is the perimeter of the figure?

b. If $Q = 3$ m, $S = 2.5$ m, and $T = 4$ m, what is the perimeter of the figure?

c. Using the variables *Q*, *S*, and *T*, write three equations for the perimeter, *P*, of the figure.

d. Using the values from part a, find the perimeter of the figure using each of your equations. Check or revise your equations if you do not get the same perimeter in each case.

e. Show that your three expressions for the perimeter are equivalent.

21. The Metropolis Middle School math and science club is planning to sell crystal-making kits to raise money for new laboratory equipment.

   a. The project will cost $4.50 per kit plus $200 for advertising. Write an equation that represents the cost, C, for k kits.

   b. The students plan to sell each kit for $12 and expect to collect an additional $225 from the kit manufacturer, who will include literature on other science products with each kit. Write an equation that represents the expected revenue, R, from selling k kits.

   c. The profit from selling the kits will be the money left after the students have deducted the cost of the kits from the revenue they collect. Write an equation that represents the profit, P, from selling k kits.

   d. How many kits will the students have to sell to break even (that is, have a profit of zero)? Explain your reasoning.

   e. How many kits will the students need to sell to raise $500?

   f. What will the profit from selling the kits be if the students sell 250 kits?

   g. How many kits will the students need to sell to raise $750?

Investigation 4

Use these problems for additional practice after Investigation 4.

In 1–10, solve the equation and check your answer.

1. $2x + 5 = 11$

2. $9 + 3x = 30$

3. $4x + 19 = 26 - 3x$

4. $x^2 - 2.5x = 0$

5. $11x - x^2 = 0$

6. $5x^2 - 2x = x^2 - 10x$

7. $3x(x - 5) = 0$

8. $4.5(x + 1) + 2(x + 1) = 0$

9. $4.5x = x - 7$

10. $81x - 9x^2 = 0$

11. At right is a graph of a parabola.

    a. What are the coordinates of the maximum or minimum point?

    b. What are the coordinates of the x-intercept(s)?

    c. What are the coordinates of the y-intercept(s)?

    d. Could $y = -(x - 4)^2 + 2$ be the equation of the parabola? Explain why or why not.

    e. Could $y = x - 2$ be the equation of the parabola? Explain why or why not.

    f. Does the line $y = -6$ intersect the parabola? Explain why or why not.

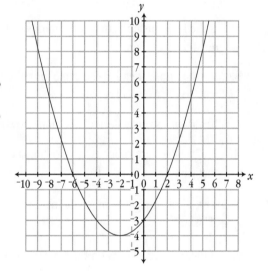

12. The profit, P, from a car wash held by the Metropolis Middle School band depends on the number of cars, C, that drive by the corner where the car wash is operated. Past experience suggests that the equation modeling the situation is approximately $P = 0.001C(C - 5)$.

    a. What profit can be expected if 100 cars drive by?

    b. What profit can be expected if 1000 cars drive by?

    c. What profit can be expected if no cars drive by? Explain why the profit predicted by the equation does or does not make sense.

    d. The band director estimates from past car washes that about 750 cars will drive by during the time the car wash is open. The band needs $700 to fund a trip to the state competition. About how many times will they have to hold the car wash to raise the necessary funds? Explain your reasoning.

13. The height in meters of a model rocket t seconds after it is launched is approximated by the equation $b = t(50 - 3t)$.

    a. How high is the rocket 5 seconds after being launched?

    b. How high is the rocket 10 seconds after being launched?

    c. Based on your answers to parts a and b, did the rocket's height continue to increase after the first 5 seconds? Explain your reasoning.

    d. What is the height of the rocket after 17 seconds? What can you conclude from your answer? Explain your reasoning.

14. At Metropolis Middle School, the number of cans, N, collected for recycling after a basketball game depends on the number of people, P, who attend the game. The approximate relationship is given by $N = 2.5(P - 40) - 100$.

    a. Is the relationship between the number of cans collected and the number of people attending linear or quadratic? Explain.

    b. If 400 people attended the game for the semifinals of the district championship, how many cans would you expect to be collected?

    c. If 300 cans were collected at a game, how many people would you expect to have attended the game?

    d. If 675 cans were collected at another game, how many people would you expect to have attended that game?

15. The cost, C, of each uniform for the players on an N-person basketball team is given by the equation $C = \frac{(40N + 260)}{N}$.

    a. If there are 25 players on the team, what is the cost of each uniform?

    b. If the cost of each uniform is $53, how many players are on the basketball team?

    c. If the cost of each uniform is $56.25, how many players are on the basketball team?

16. The sum of the length and width of a rectangle is 20 meters. The area of the rectangle is given by the equation $A = w(20 - w)$, where w is the width.

    a. What is the area of the rectangle if the width is 2 meters?

    b. What is the area of the rectangle if the length is 8 meters? Show how you found your answer.

    c. Suppose the area of the rectangle is 75 square meters. What is the width of the rectangle? What is the length of the rectangle?

    d. Suppose the area of the rectangle is 96 square meters. What is the width of the rectangle? What is the length of the rectangle?

    e. What are the dimensions of the rectangle if its area is 93.75 square meters?

© Prentice-Hall, Inc.

Investigation 5

Use these problems for additional practice after Investigation 5.

1. Toothpicks were used to make the pattern below.

   1st   2nd   3rd   4th

   a. How many toothpicks will be in the 5th figure? In the 6th figure?

   b. Write an equation for the number of toothpicks, *t,* needed to make the *n*th figure.

   c. Identify and describe the figure in this pattern that can be made with exactly 100 toothpicks.

2. Toothpicks were used to make the pattern below.

   1st   2nd   3rd   4th

   a. How many toothpicks will be in the 5th figure? In the 6th figure?

   b. Write an equation for the number of toothpicks, *t,* needed to make the *n*th figure.

   c. Identify and describe the figure in this pattern that can be made with exactly 61 toothpicks.

3. Square tiles were used to make the pattern below.

   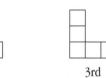

   1st   2nd   3rd   4th

   a. How many tiles will be in the 5th figure? In the 6th figure?

   b. Write an equation for the number of tiles, *t,* needed to make the *n*th figure.

   c. Identify and describe the figure in this pattern that can be made with exactly 25 tiles.

4. Square tiles were used to make the pattern below.

     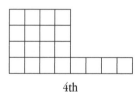

   1st   2nd   3rd   4th

   a. How many tiles will be in the 5th figure? In the 6th figure?

   b. Write an equation for the number of tiles, *t,* needed to make the *n*th figure.

   c. Identify and describe the figure in this pattern that can be made with exactly 420 tiles.

Blackline Masters

and Additional Practice

for *Kaleidoscopes, Hubcaps, and Mirrors*

Problem 1.1

A.

B.

C.    D.

Problem 1.2

hubcap 1

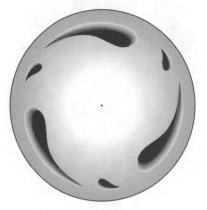

hubcap 2

hubcap 3

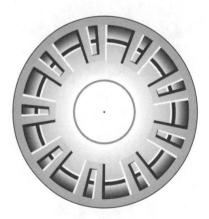

hubcap 4

Problem 1.3

design 1

design 2

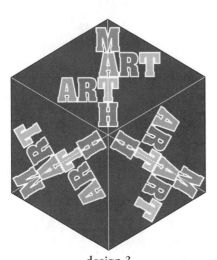

design 3

design 4

design 5

design 6

Problem 1.4

tessellation 1

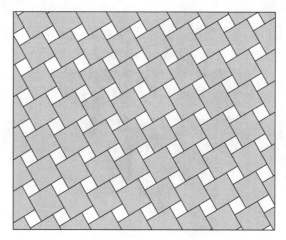

tessellation 2

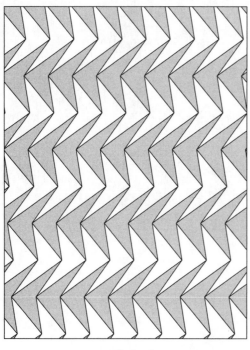

tessellation 3

tessellation 4

ACE Questions 1–3

1.

2.

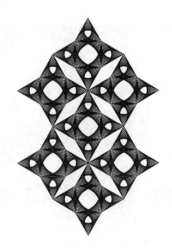

3.

ACE Questions 4–8

4.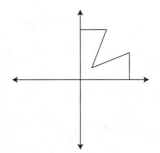

5. COOKIE

6.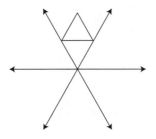

7. 1 2 3 4 5 6 7 8 9 0

8.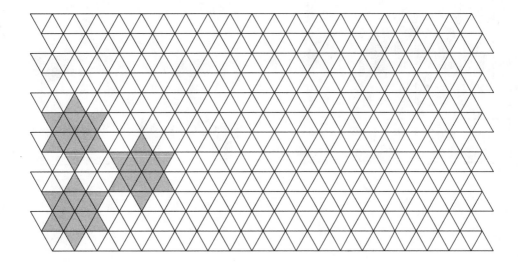

ACE Questions 9–12

9.

10.

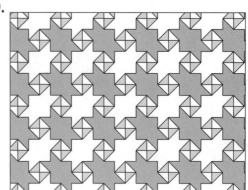

11.

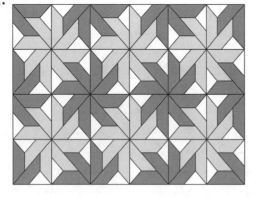

12.

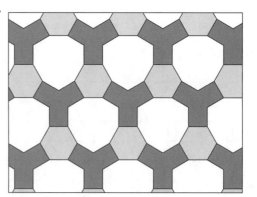

ACE Questions 20–23

20.

21.

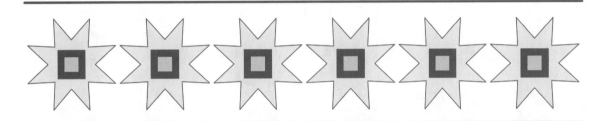

22.

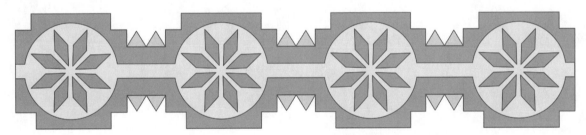

23.

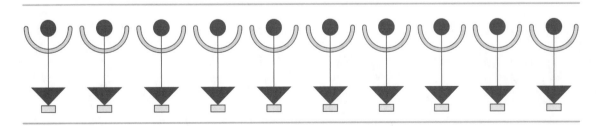

Problem 2.1

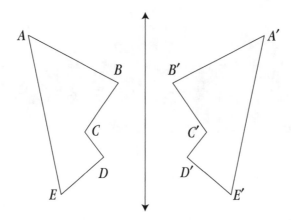

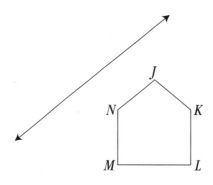

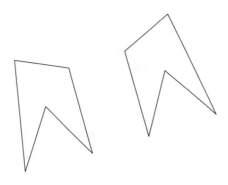

Problem 2.1 Follow-Up

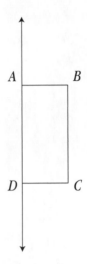

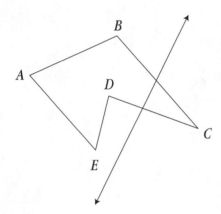

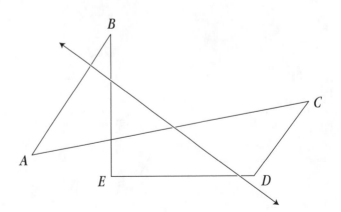

Problem 2.2 and Follow-Up

diagram 1

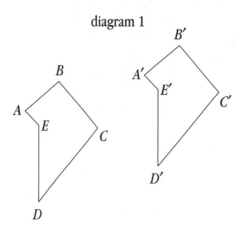

diagram 2

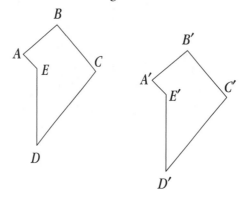

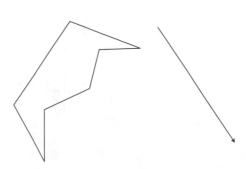

Problem 2.3

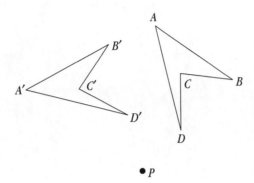

• *P*

Rotate 90° about point *P*.

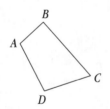

• *P*

Rotate 45° about point *Q*.

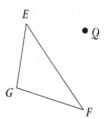

• *Q*

Problem 2.3 Follow-Up

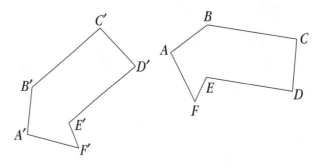

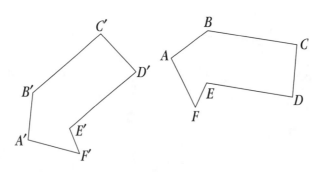

Problem 2.4

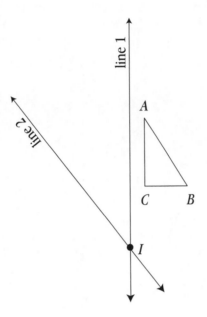

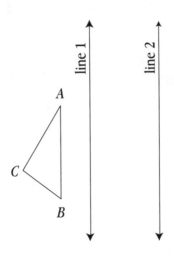

Problem 2.4 Follow-Up

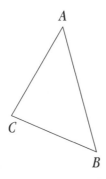

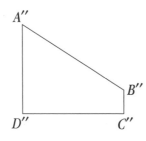

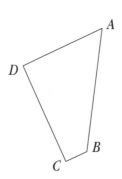

ACE Questions 1–4

1.

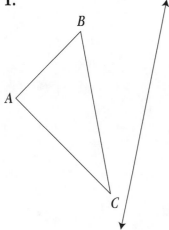

2.

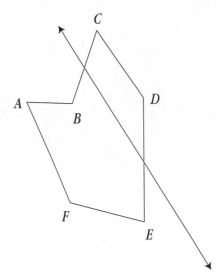

3.

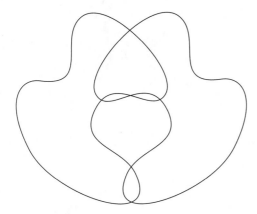

4.

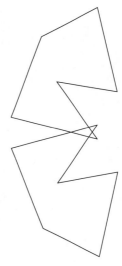

ACE Questions 5–8

5.

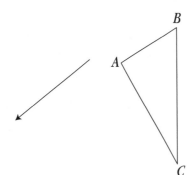

7.

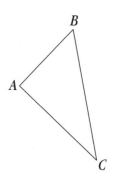

6.

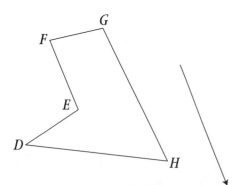

8.

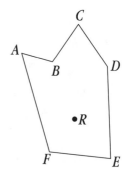

ACE Questions 9–11

9.

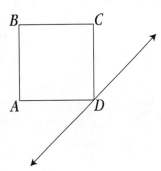

10.

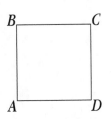

11.

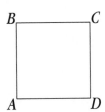

•D'

ACE Questions 12–15

12.

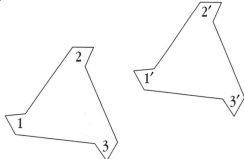

13.

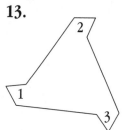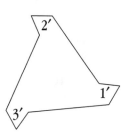

14.

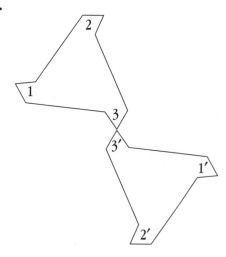

15.

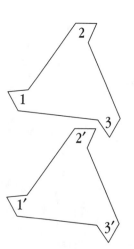

Problem 3.1

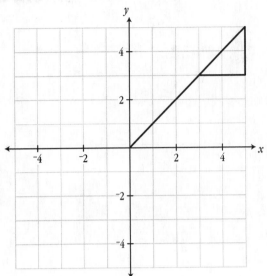

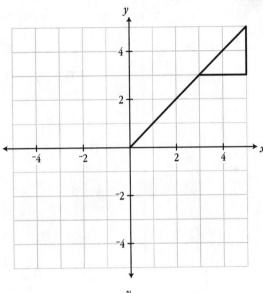

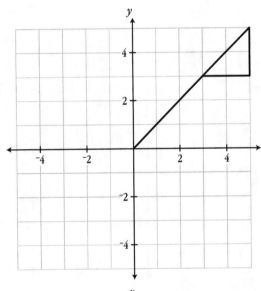

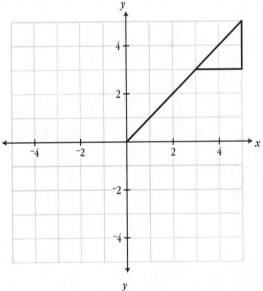

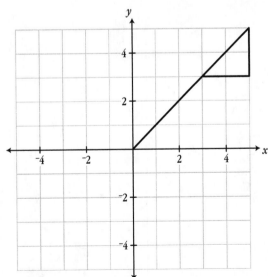

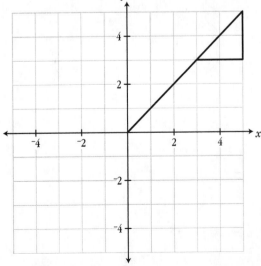

Kaleidoscopes, Hubcaps, and Mirrors

Problem 3.1 Follow-Up

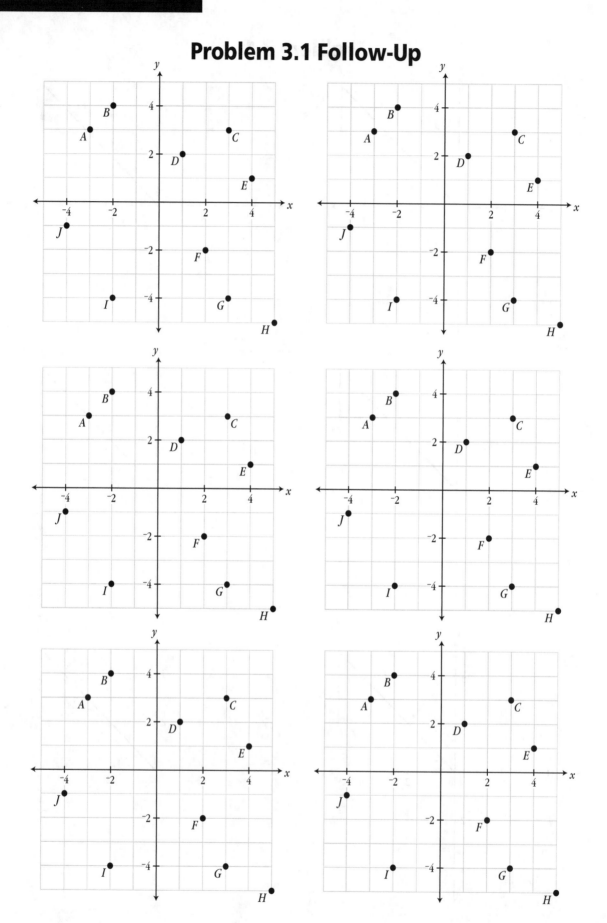

Problem 3.3

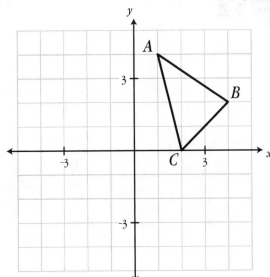

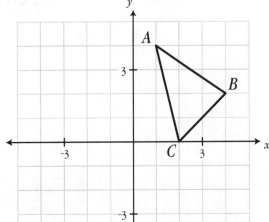

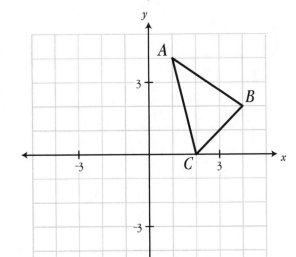

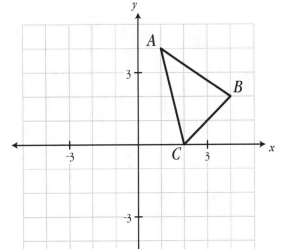

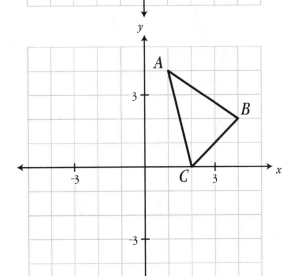

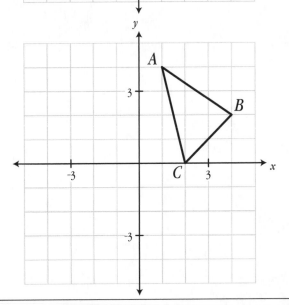

Problem 3.4

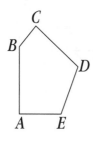 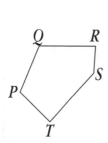 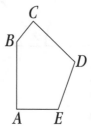

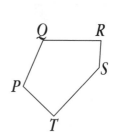

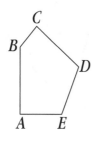 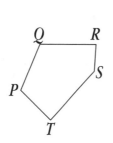 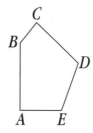

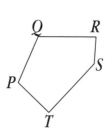

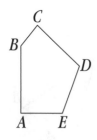 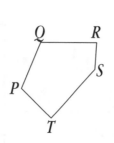 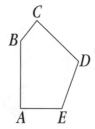

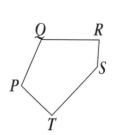

ACE Questions 1–3 and 6–15

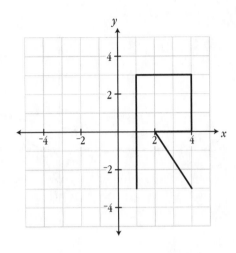

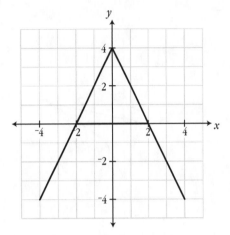

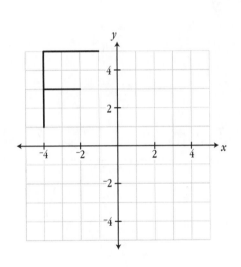

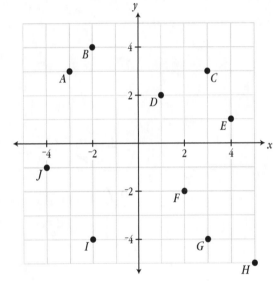

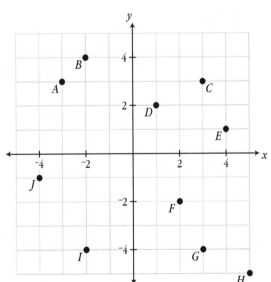

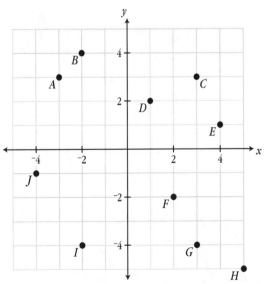

ACE Questions 16 and 24–26

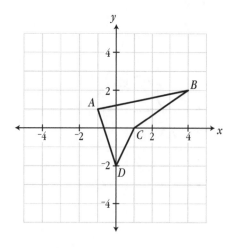

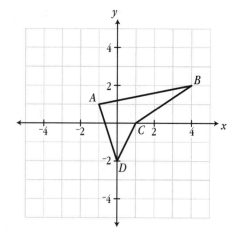

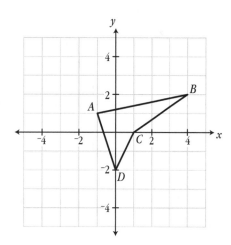

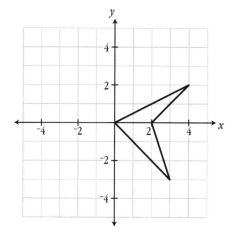

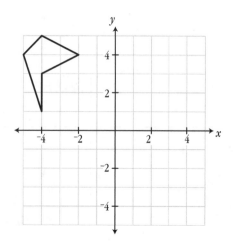

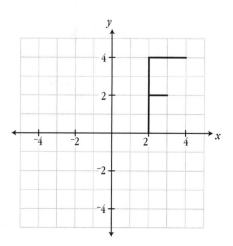

ACE Question 27

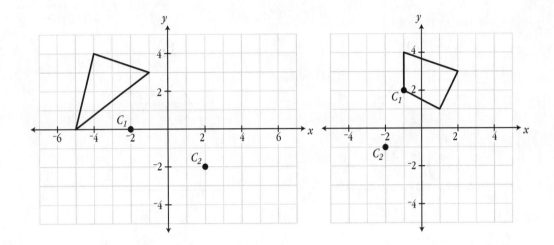

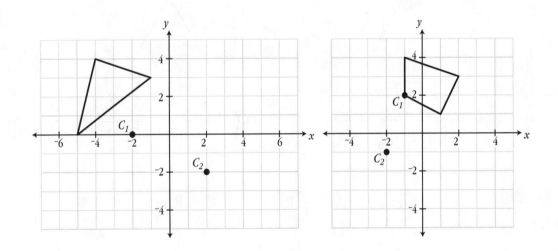

Symmetry Transformations on an Equilateral Triangle

L_1

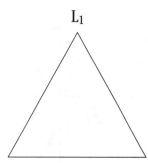

L_2

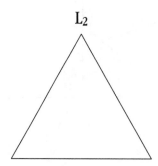

L_3

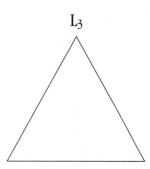

R_{360}

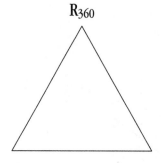

R_{120}

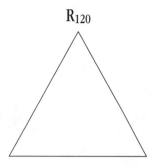

R_{240}

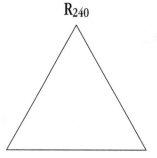

Problem 4.1

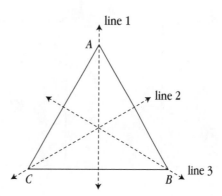

✳	R_{360}	R_{120}	R_{240}	L_1	L_2	L_3
R_{360}						
R_{120}						
R_{240}						
L_1					R_{240}	
L_2						
L_3		L_2				

×	1	2	3	4	5	6
1						
2						
3						
4						
5						
6						

Labsheet 4.2A

Symmetry Transformations on a Square

L_1

L_2

L_3

L_4

R_{360}

R_{90}

R_{180}

R_{270}

Problem 4.2

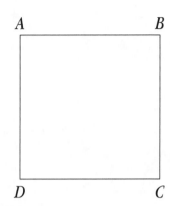

✳	R_{360}							
R_{360}								

×	1	2	3	4	5	6		
1								
2								
3								
4								
5								
6								
7								
8								

ACE Question 8

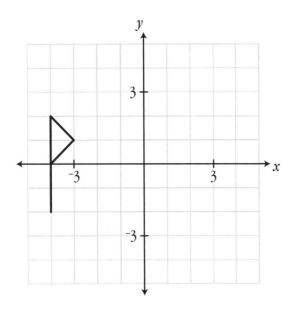

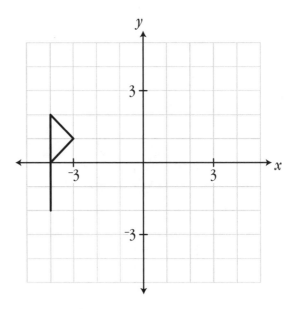

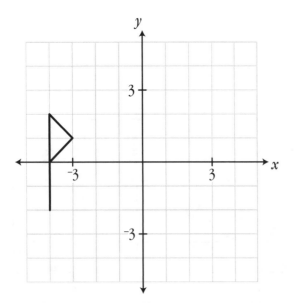

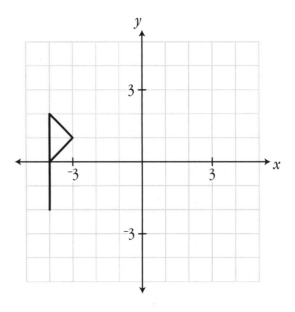

The designs below are reproduced on Labsheet 1.1. Use mirrors, tracing paper, or other tools to help you find all the lines of symmetry in each design.

A.

B.

C.

D.

The pinwheel design below has *rotational symmetry.* It can be rotated 45°, 90°, 135°, 180°, 225°, 270°, 315°, or 360° about its centerpoint to a position in which it looks the same as the original design.

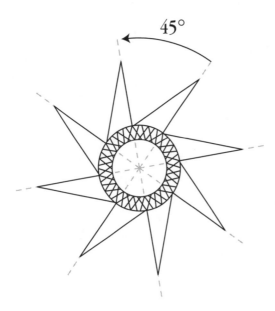

The *angle of rotation* is the smallest angle through which a design can be rotated to coincide with the original design. The angle of rotation for this pinwheel is 45°. Notice that the other rotation angles are multiples of 45°.

Rotational symmetry can be found in many objects that rotate about a centerpoint. For example, the automobile hubcaps shown below have rotational symmetry.

A. Determine the angle of rotation for each hubcap. Explain how you found the angle.

B. Some of the hubcaps also have reflectional symmetry. Sketch all the lines of symmetry for each hubcap.

hubcap 1

hubcap 2

hubcap 3

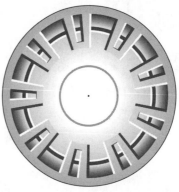

hubcap 4

Do parts A and B for each kaleidoscope design.

A. Look for reflectional symmetry in each design. Sketch all the lines of symmetry you find.

B. Look for rotational symmetry in each design. Determine the angle of rotation for each design.

design 1

design 2

design 3

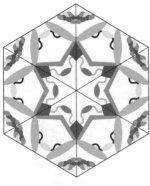

design 4

design 5

design 6

Each tessellation below has translational symmetry. Do parts A and B for each tessellation.

A. Outline a basic design element that could be used to create the tessellation using only translations.

B. Write directions or draw an arrow showing how the basic design element can be copied and slid to produce another part of the pattern.

9.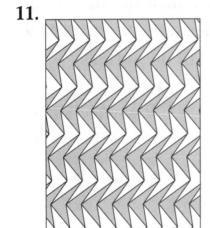

10.

11.

12.

A. Polygon $A'B'C'D'E'$ is the image of polygon $ABCDE$ under a line reflection.

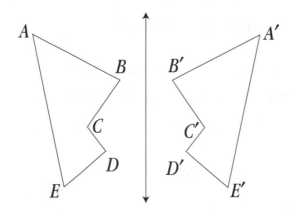

1. Draw a line segment from each vertex of polygon $ABCDE$ to its image on polygon $A'B'C'D'E'$.

2. Measure the angles formed by each segment you drew and the line of reflection.

3. For each vertex of polygon $ABCDE$, measure the distance from the vertex to the line of reflection and the distance from the line of reflection to the image of the vertex.

4. Describe the patterns in your measurements from parts 2 and 3.

B. Use what you discovered in part A to draw the image of polygon *JKLMN* under a reflection. Use only a pencil, a ruler, and an angle ruler or protractor. Describe how you drew the image.

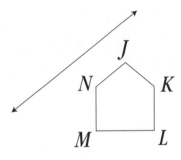

C. Use only a pencil, a ruler, and an angle ruler or protractor to find the line of symmetry for the design below. Describe how you found the line of symmetry.

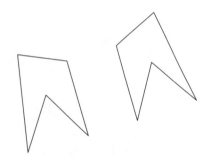

D. Complete this definition of a line reflection: A *line reflection* matches each point *X* on a figure to an image point *X′* so that . . .

A. Each diagram below shows polygon *ABCDE* and its image under a translation. These figures are reproduced on Labsheet 2.2. Do parts 1 and 2 for each diagram.

diagram 1

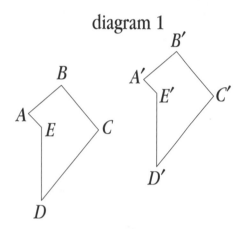

diagram 2

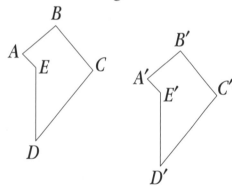

1. Draw a line segment from each vertex of polygon *ABCDE* to its image.

2. Describe the relationship among the line segments you drew.

B. The translations in part A slide polygon *ABCDE* onto its image, polygon *A′B′C′D′E′*. Do parts 1–3 for each diagram in part A.

1. By performing the same translation that was used to slide polygon *ABCDE* to polygon *A′B′C′D′E′*, slide polygon *A′B′C′D′E′* to create a new image. Label the image *A″B″C″D″E″*.

2. Polygon *A″B″C″D″E″* is the image of polygon *ABCDE* after two identical translations. How is polygon *A″B″C″D″E″* related to polygon *ABCDE*?

3. Does your final drawing of the three figures have translational symmetry? Explain.

C. Complete this definition of a translation: A *translation* matches any two points *X* and *Y* on a figure to image points *X′* and *Y′* so that . . .

A. Polygon $A'B'C'D'$ is the image of polygon $ABCD$ under a rotation of $60°$ about point P. We call point P the *center of rotation*.

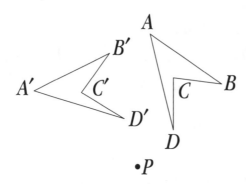

1. What relationship would you expect to find between each vertex, its image, and point P?

2. For each vertex of polygon $ABCD$, find the measure of the angle formed by the vertex, point P, and the image of the vertex. For example, find the measure of angle APA'.

3. For each vertex of polygon $ABCD$, find the distance from the vertex to point P and the distance from the image of the vertex to point P. For example, find AP and $A'P$.

4. What patterns do you see in your measurements? Do these patterns confirm the conjecture you made in part 1?

B. Do parts 1 and 2 for each figure below.

    1. Perform the indicated rotation, and label the image vertices.

    2. Describe the path each vertex follows under the rotation.

       Rotate 90° about point *P*.   Rotate 45° about point *Q*.

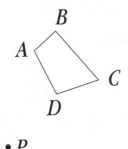
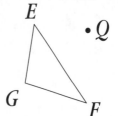

C. For the figures in part B, use the specified rotation to rotate the *image* of the original polygon. The result is the image of the original polygon after two identical rotations. How does the location of the final image compare with the location of the original polygon? Be very specific.

D. Complete this definition of a rotation: A rotation of *d* degrees about a point *P* matches any point *X* on a figure to an image point *X'* so that . . .

A. 1. The figure below is reproduced on Labsheet 2.4A. Reflect triangle *ABC* over line 1. Then reflect the image over line 2. Label the final image *A″B″C″*.

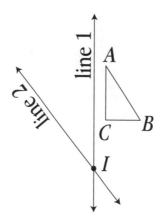

2. For each vertex of triangle *ABC*, measure the angle formed by the vertex, point *I*, and the image of the vertex. For example, measure angle *AIA″*. What do you observe?

3. For each vertex of triangle *ABC*, compare the distance from the vertex to point *I* with the distance from the image of the vertex to point *I*. What do you observe?

4. Could you move triangle *ABC* to triangle *A″B″C″* with a single transformation? If so, describe the transformation.

5. Make a conjecture about the result of reflecting a figure over two intersecting lines. Test your conjecture with an example.

B. 1. What will happen if you reflect a figure over a line and then reflect the image over a second line that is *parallel* to the first line? Would the combination of the two reflections be equivalent to a single transformation?

2. Test your conjecture from part 1 on several examples, including the one shown here. Do the results support your conjecture? If so, explain why. If not, revise your conjecture to better explain your results.

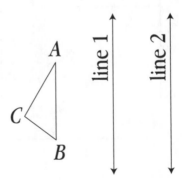

The drawing screen in many computer geometry programs is considered to be a coordinate grid. You can create designs by specifying the endpoints of line segments.

The flag below consists of three segments. The commands for creating the flag tell the computer to draw segments between the specified endpoints.

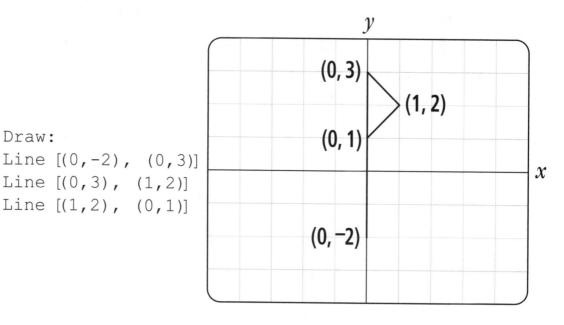

```
Draw:
Line [(0,-2), (0,3)]
Line [(0,3), (1,2)]
Line [(1,2), (0,1)]
```

Is there a different set of commands that would create the same flag?

What commands would create a square centered at the origin?

What commands would create a nonsquare rectangle?

A. Copy and complete the commands to create a set of instructions for drawing the flag below.

```
Draw:
Line [(   ,   ), (   ,   )]
Line [(   ,   ), (   ,   )]
Line [(   ,   ), (   ,   )]
```

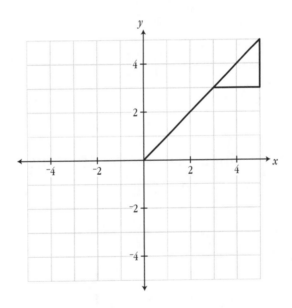

B. Write a set of commands that would draw the image of this flag under a reflection over the *y*-axis.

```
Draw:
Line [(   ,   ), (   ,   )]
Line [(   ,   ), (   ,   )]
Line [(   ,   ), (   ,   )]
```

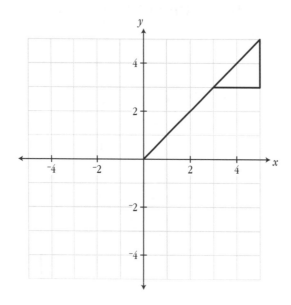

C. Write a set of commands that would draw the image of this flag under a reflection over the *x*-axis.
   ```
   Draw:
   Line [(   ,   ), (   ,   )]
   Line [(   ,   ), (   ,   )]
   Line [(   ,   ), (   ,   )]
   ```

D. Write a set of commands that would draw the image of this flag under a reflection over the line *y* = *x*.
   ```
   Draw:
   Line [(   ,   ), (   ,   )]
   Line [(   ,   ), (   ,   )]
   Line [(   ,   ), (   ,   )]
   ```

A. 1. In diagram 1, the left-most flag can be drawn with these commands:

```
Draw:
Line [(−5,−4), (−5,2)]
Line [(−5,2), (−4,1)]
Line [(−4,1), (−5,0)]
```

This draws the vertical segment, then the upper slanted segment, and finally the lower slanted segment.

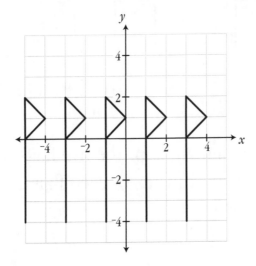

Write sets of commands for drawing the other four flags in diagram 1. Each set of commands should draw the segments in the same order as the commands for the original flag.

Flag 2
```
Draw:
Line [(  ,  ), (  ,  )]
Line [(  ,  ), (  ,  )]
Line [(  ,  ), (  ,  )]
```

Flag 3
```
Draw:
Line [(  ,  ), (  ,  )]
Line [(  ,  ), (  ,  )]
Line [(  ,  ), (  ,  )]
```

Flag 4
```
Draw:
Line [(  ,  ), (  ,  )]
Line [(  ,  ), (  ,  )]
Line [(  ,  ), (  ,  )]
```

Flag 5
```
Draw:
Line [(  ,  ), (  ,  )]
Line [(  ,  ), (  ,  )]
Line [(  ,  ), (  ,  )]
```

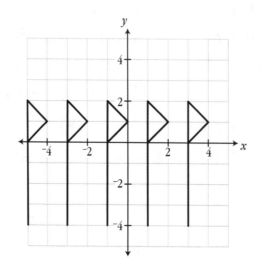

A. 2. Compare the commands for the five flags. Describe a pattern that relates the coordinates of each flag to the coordinates of the flag to its *right*.

```
Draw:
Line [( , ), ( , )]
Line [( , ), ( , )]
Line [( , ), ( , )]
```

3. Describe a pattern that relates the coordinates of each flag to the coordinates of the flag to its *left*.

```
Draw:
Line [( , ), ( , )]
Line [( , ), ( , )]
Line [( , ), ( , )]
```

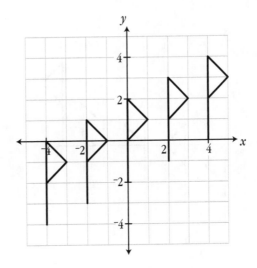

B. 1. Write a set of commands for drawing the left-most flag in diagram 2. Then write comparable instructions for drawing the other four flags.

Flag 1
Draw:
Line [(,), (,)]
Line [(,), (,)]
Line [(,), (,)]

Flag 2
Draw:
Line [(,), (,)]
Line [(,), (,)]
Line [(,), (,)]

Flag 3
Draw:
Line [(,), (,)]
Line [(,), (,)]
Line [(,), (,)]

Flag 4
Draw:
Line [(,), (,)]
Line [(,), (,)]
Line [(,), (,)]

Flag 5
Draw:
Line [(,), (,)]
Line [(,), (,)]
Line [(,), (,)]

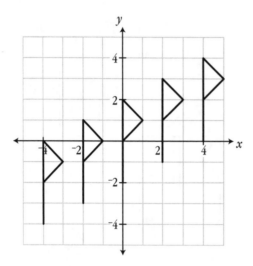

B. 2. Compare the commands for the five flags. Describe a pattern that relates the coordinates of each flag to the coordinates of the flag to its *right*.

3. Describe a pattern that relates the coordinates of each flag to the coordinates of the flag to its *left*.

A. Copy and complete the commands to create a set of instructions for drawing triangle *ABC*.

```
Draw:
Line [( , ), ( , )]
Line [( , ), ( , )]
Line [( , ), ( , )]
```

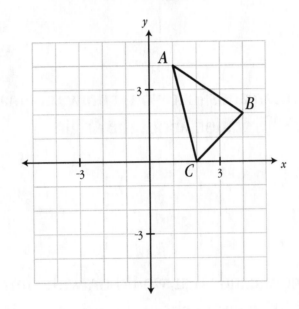

B. Write a set of commands that would draw the image of triangle *ABC* under a 90° rotation about the origin.

```
Draw:
Line [( , ), ( , )]
Line [( , ), ( , )]
Line [( , ), ( , )]
```

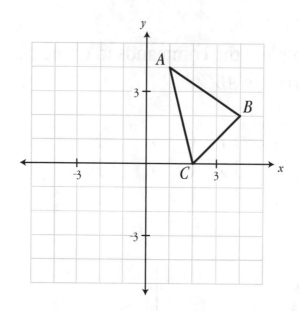

C. Write a set of commands that would draw the image of triangle *ABC* under a 180° rotation about the origin.

```
Draw:
Line [(   ,   ), (   ,   )]
Line [(   ,   ), (   ,   )]
Line [(   ,   ), (   ,   )]
```

D. Write a set of commands that would draw the image of triangle *ABC* under a 270° rotation about the origin.

```
Draw:
Line [(   ,   ), (   ,   )]
Line [(   ,   ), (   ,   )]
Line [(   ,   ), (   ,   )]
```

E. Write a set of commands that would draw the image of triangle *ABC* under a 360° rotation about the origin.

```
Draw:
Line [(   ,   ), (   ,   )]
Line [(   ,   ), (   ,   )]
Line [(   ,   ), (   ,   )]
```

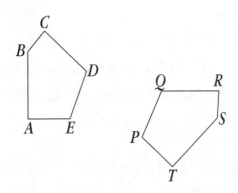

A. If you made a copy of one of the pentagons and fit it exactly on the other, which vertices would match?

B. Which pairs of sides in pentagons *ABCDE* and *PQRST* are the same length?

C. Which pairs of angles in pentagons *ABCDE* and *PQRST* are the same size?

D. What combination of reflections, rotations, and translations would move pentagon *ABCDE* to fit exactly on pentagon *PQRST*? Is there more than one possible combination? Make sketches to show your ideas.

Complete the table to show the results of combining symmetry transformations of an equilateral triangle. Each entry should be the result of performing the transformation in the left column followed by the transformation in the top row.

The two entries already in the table represent the combinations you explored in the introduction:

$$L_1 * L_2 = R_{240} \qquad\qquad L_3 * R_{120} = L_2$$

$*$	R_{360}	R_{120}	R_{240}	L_1	L_2	L_3
R_{360}						
R_{120}						
R_{240}						
L_1					R_{240}	
L_2						
L_3		L_2				

Note that transformation R_{360}, a 360° rotation, carries every point back to where it started. As you combine transformations, you will discover that many combinations are equivalent to R_{360}.

A. On Labsheet 4.2B, draw all the lines of symmetry and describe all the rotations that produce images that exactly match the original square. Label the lines of symmetry in clockwise order as line 1, line 2, and so on.

B. Cut out a copy of the square, and copy each vertex label onto the back side of the square. Use this copy to explore combinations of symmetry transformations. Complete the operation table to show the results of combining pairs of transformations. When you enter the column heads, first list the rotations and then the reflections. Use the same order for the row heads.

✳	R_{360}							
R_{360}								

The operations of addition and multiplication satisfy important properties that are useful for reasoning about expressions and equations.

- The order in which numbers are added or multiplied does not affect the result. This is called the commutative property. We say that addition and multiplication are *commutative operations.* In symbols, if a and b are real numbers, then

$$a + b = b + a \quad \text{and} \quad a \times b = b \times a.$$

- Adding 0 to a number has no effect. Multiplying a number by 1 has no effect. In symbols, if a is a real number, then

$$0 + a = a + 0 = a \quad \text{and} \quad 1 \times a = a \times 1 = a.$$

We call 0 and 1 *identity elements;* 0 is the additive identity, and 1 is the multiplicative identity.

- For any number a, the sum of a and $-a$ is 0, the additive identity. For any nonzero number a, the product of a and $\frac{1}{a}$ is 1, the multiplicative identity.

$$a + -a = -a + a = 0 \quad \text{and} \quad a \times \frac{1}{a} = \frac{1}{a} \times a = 1$$

We call $-a$ the *additive inverse* of a and $\frac{1}{a}$ the *multiplicative inverse* of a.

Refer to your operation table for combining symmetry transformations for an equilateral triangle.

A. Is ✳ a commutative operation? In other words, does the order in which you combine symmetry transformations make a difference? Justify your answer.

B. Like addition and multiplication, the ✳ operation has an identity element. That is, there is a transformation that has no effect when it is applied before or after another transformation. Tell which transformation is the identity element, and explain how you know.

C. Does each symmetry transformation have an inverse? That is, can you combine each transformation with another transformation, in either order, to get the identity element you found in part B? If so, list each transformation and its inverse.

Dear Family,

We can see symmetry all around us, in designs on gift wrap and fabrics and pottery. Symmetry can be over a line, as we see in a kite or a butterfly. Symmetry can be about a point, as in pinwheels and hubcaps. And it can be in a strip pattern such as those often seen on wallpaper borders. The late Dutch artist M. C. Escher (1898–1972) is famous for the use of symmetry in his artwork.

The next unit your child will be studying in mathematics class this year involves the geometry of symmetry and the kinds of motion that can be used to create symmetrical designs. *Kaleidoscopes, Hubcaps, and Mirrors* is an introduction to the topic in mathematics called *transformational geometry*.

We often think of algebra and geometry as two different branches of mathematics. In this unit, students will see some of the many ways in which algebra and geometry complement and reinforce each other.

Here are some strategies for helping your child during this unit:

- Talk with your child about the ideas presented in the text about symmetry. Look with your child for examples of each type of symmetry.

- Talk with your child about careers that use the knowledge of geometry, such as crystallography, a science that deals with the forms and structures of crystals.

- Encourage your child's efforts in completing all homework assignments.

As always, if you have any questions or suggestions about your child's mathematics program, please feel free to call. We are interested in your child and want to be sure this year's mathematics experiences are enjoyable and promote a firm understanding of mathematics.

Sincerely,

Estimada familia,

La simetría está presente en todo nuestro entorno, en los dibujos que aparecen en el papel de envolver regalos, en los tejidos y en la cerámica. La simetría puede presentarse con respecto a una recta, como ocurre con las cometas o las mariposas. También puede darse con respecto a un punto, como es el caso de los molinetes y los tapacubos. E incluso puede presentarse la simetría en los patrones de las bandas decorativas como, por ejemplo, en los que aparecen frecuentemente en los frisos del papel de empapelar. El fallecido artista holandés M. C. Escher (1898–1972) es famoso por utilizar en sus obras la simetría.

La próxima unidad que su hijo o hija estudiará este año en la clase de matemáticas trata sobre la geometría de la simetría y sobre los tipos de movimientos que pueden emplearse para crear diseños simétricos. *Kaleidoscopes, Hubcaps, and Mirrors* (Calidoscopios, tapacubos, y espejos) sirve de introducción al tema matemático llamado *geometría de transformaciones.*

Muchas veces consideramos al álgebra y a la geometría como a dos ramas diferentes de las matemáticas. En esta unidad los alumnos conocerán algunas de las diversas maneras en que el álgebra y la geometría se complementan y se refuerzan mutuamente.

He aquí algunas estrategias que ustedes pueden emplear para ayudar a su hijo o hija en esta unidad:

- Comenten con él o ella las ideas que se presentan en el texto en relación a la simetría. Busquen ejemplos de cada uno de los tipos de simetría.

- Hablen juntos sobre las profesiones en las que se emplean conocimientos geométricos, como puede ser en la cristalografía, la ciencia que estudia las formas y las estructuras de los cristales.

- Animen a su hijo o hija a esforzarse para que complete toda la tarea.

Y como de costumbre, si ustedes tienen alguna duda o recomendación relacionada con el programa de matemáticas de su hijo o hija, no duden en llamarnos. Nos interesa su hijo o hija y queremos asegurarnos de que las experiencias matemáticas que tenga este año sean lo más amenas posibles y ayuden a fomentar en él o ella una sólida comprensión de las matemáticas.

Atentamente,

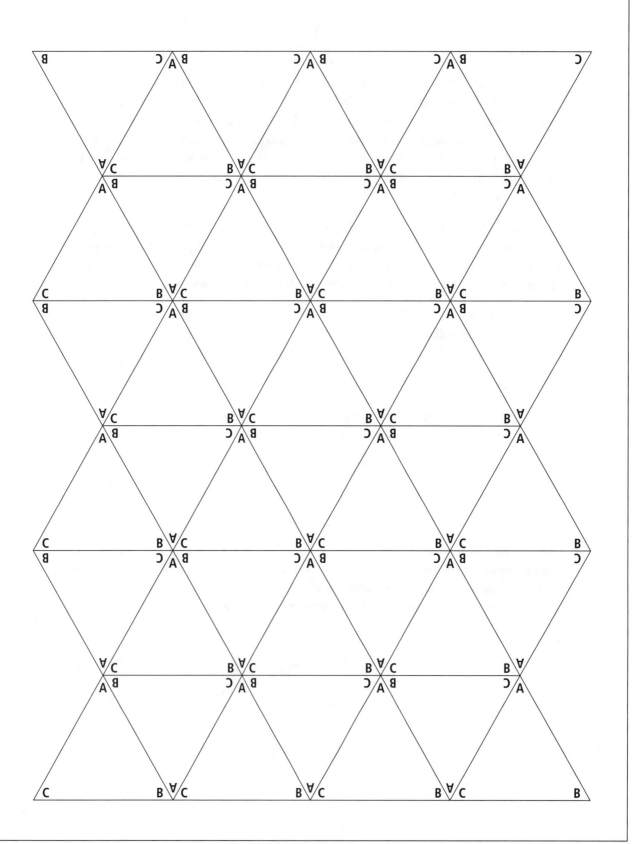

A	B	A	B	A	B	A	B
C	D	C	D	C	D	C	D

A	B	A	B	A	B	A	B
C	D	C	D	C	D	C	D

A	B	A	B	A	B	A	B
C	D	C	D	C	D	C	D

A	B	A	B	A	B	A	B
C	D	C	D	C	D	C	D

A	B	A	B	A	B	A	B
C	D	C	D	C	D	C	D

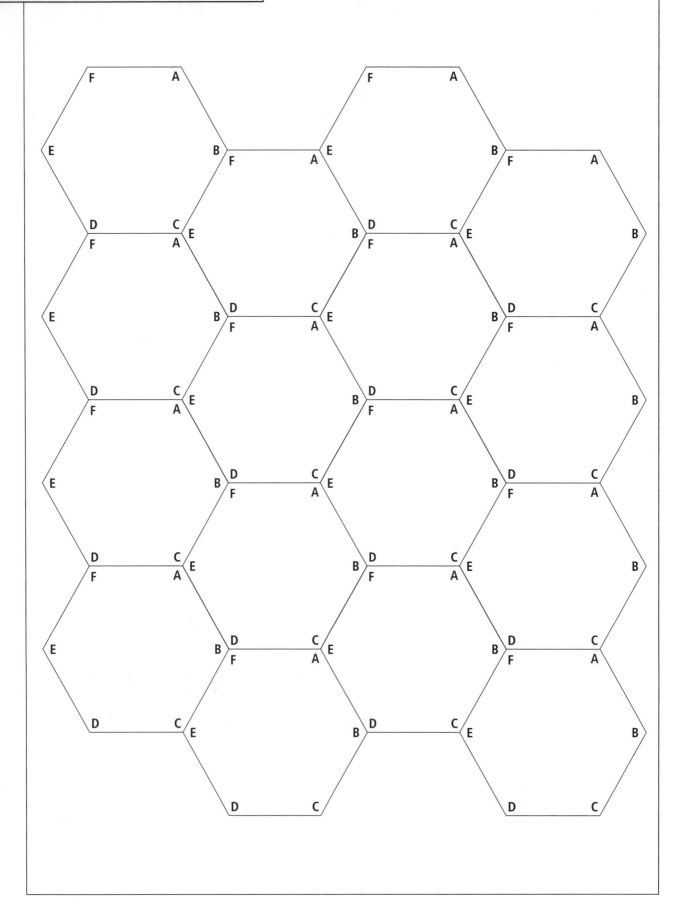

Kaleidoscopes, Hubcaps, and Mirrors

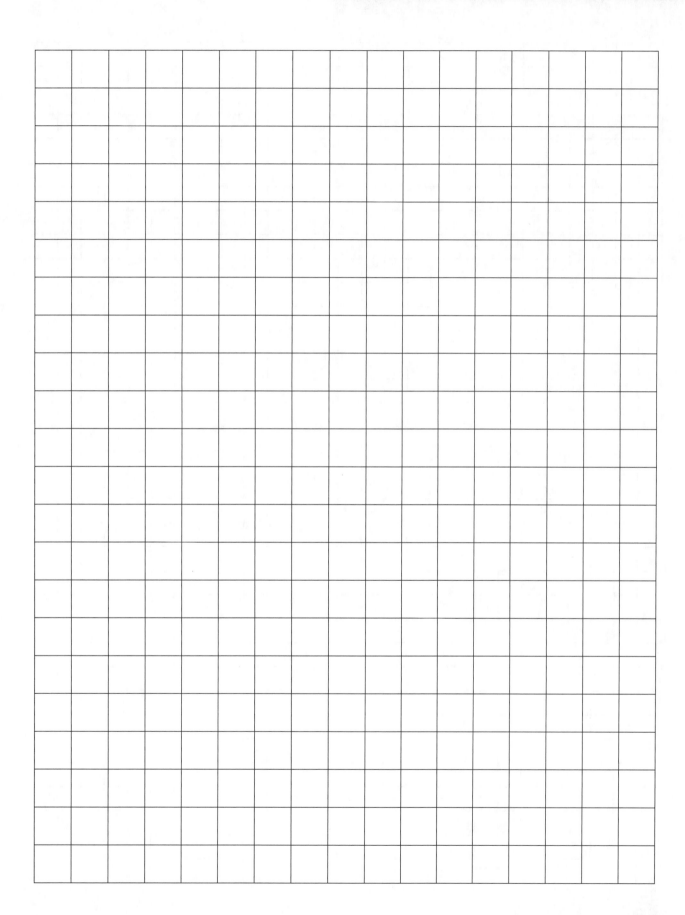

Quarter-Inch Grid Paper

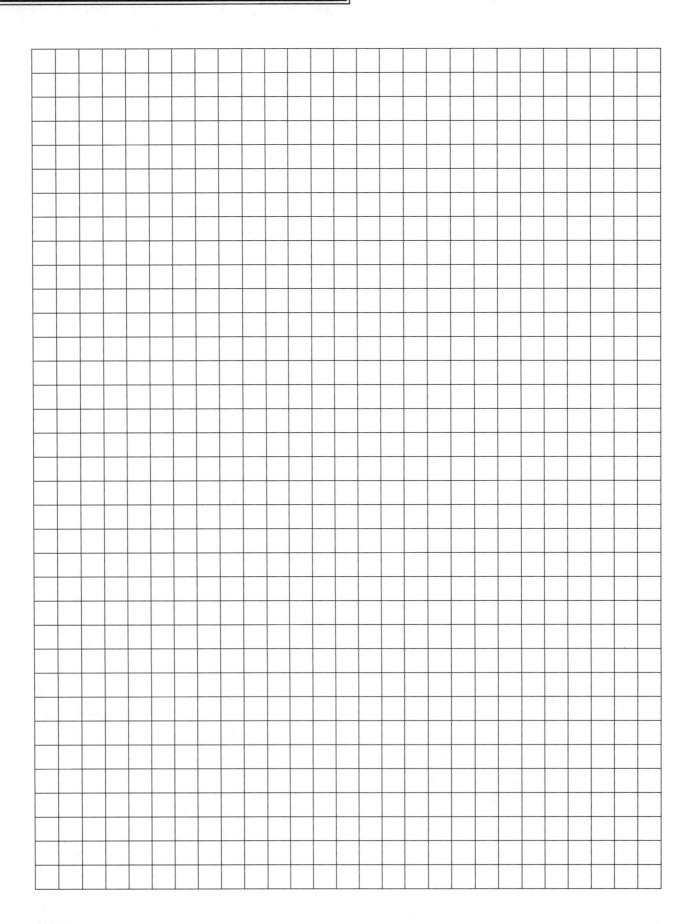

© Prentice-Hall, Inc.

Investigation 1

Use these problems for additional practice after Investigation 1.

In 1–6, determine all the types of symmetry in the design. Specify lines of symmetry, centers and angles of rotation, and lengths and directions of translations.

1.

2.

3.

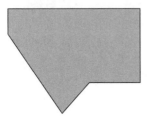

4.

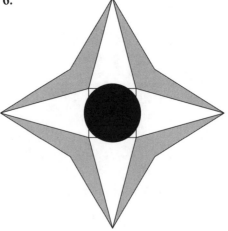

5.

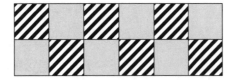

6.

© Prentice-Hall, Inc.

In 7 and 8, a basic design element and one or more lines are given. Use the basic design element to create a design with the given lines as lines of symmetry.

7.

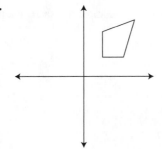

8.

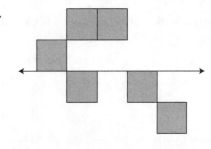

In 9 and 10, indicate the lines of symmetry and the center and angle of rotation for the line design.

9.

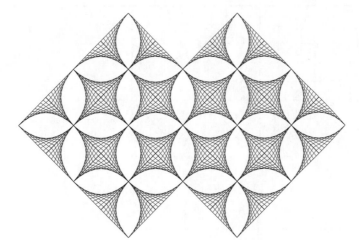

10.

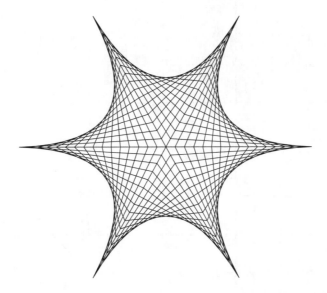

Source: Dale Seymour. *Introduction to Line Designs.* Palo Alto, Calif.: Dale Seymour Publications, 1992.

Investigation 2

Use these problems for additional practice after Investigation 2.

In 1 and 2, describe a reflection or a combination of two reflections that would move shape 1 to exactly match shape 2.

1.

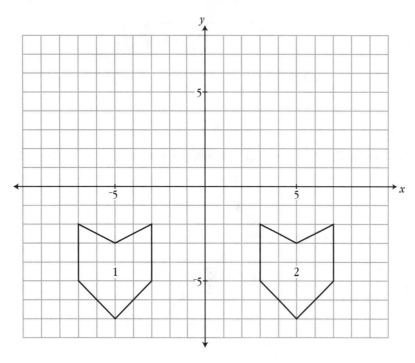

2.

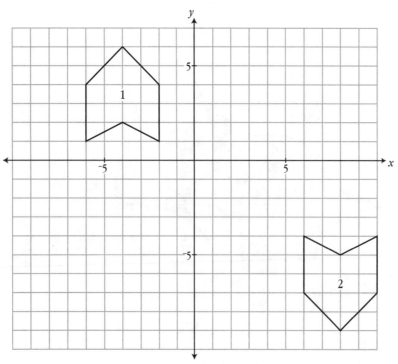

In 3 and 4, draw the image of the polygon under a reflection over the line. Describe what happens to each point on the original polygon under the reflection.

3.

4.

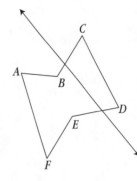

In 5 and 6, a shape and its image under a line reflection are given. Do parts a and b.

5.

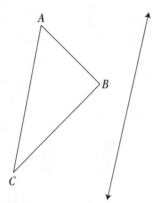

6.

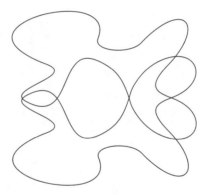

a. Draw the line of symmetry for the figure.

b. Label three points on the figure, and label the corresponding image points.

In 7 and 8, perform the translation indicated by the arrow. Describe what happens to each point of the original figure under the translation.

7.

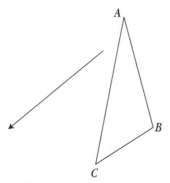

8.

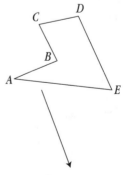

9. Rotate triangle *ABC* 90° about point *R*. Describe what happens to each point of triangle *ABC* under the rotation.

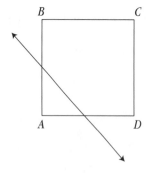

10. Rotate polygon *ABCDEF* 180° about point *F*. Describe what happens to each point of polygon *ABCDEF* under the rotation.

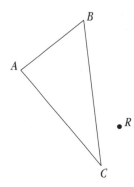

In 11–13, refer to this diagram.

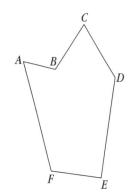

11. Draw the image of square *ABCD* under a reflection over the line.

12. Draw the image of square *ABCD* under a 45° rotation about point *D*.

13. Draw the image of square *ABCD* under the translation that slides point *D* to point *P*.

Kaleidoscopes, Hubcaps, and Mirrors

In 14–17, a polygon and its image under a transformation are given. Decide whether the transformation was a line reflection, a rotation, or a translation. Then indicate the reflection line, the center and angle of rotation, or the direction and distance of the translation.

14.

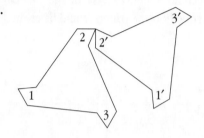

15.

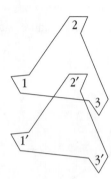

16.

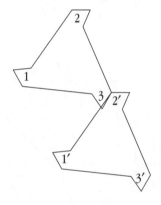

17.

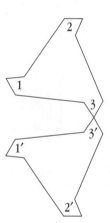

Investigation 3

Use these problems for additional practice after Investigation 3.

In 1 and 2, assume that the pattern in the graph continues in both directions. Identify a basic design element that could be copied and transformed to create the entire pattern, and describe how the pattern could be created from that design element.

1.

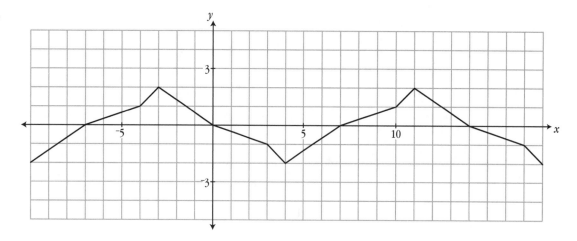

2.

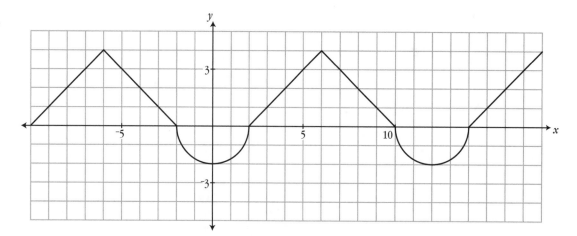

3. Plot the points (2, 4), (3, 5), (5, 5), (4, 4), (5, 3), and (3, 3) on a coordinate grid. Form a polygon by connecting the points in order and then connecting the last point to the first point. Reflect the polygon over the *y*-axis. Then translate the image 6 units to the right. Finally, rotate the second image 90° about the origin. What are the coordinates of the vertices of the final image?

4. Suppose the shape below is translated according to the rolls of a six-sided number cube.
    - If a 1, 2, or 3 is rolled, the shape is translated 3 units to the right.
    - If a 4 is rolled, the shape is translated 3 units up.
    - If a 5 is rolled, the shape is translated 3 units down.
    - If a 6 is rolled, the shape is translated 3 units to the left.

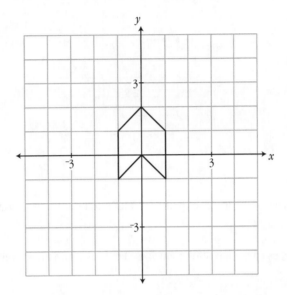

a. Draw the shape in its location after the following sequence of rolls: 3, 5, 6. What are the new coordinates of a general point (x, y) on the shape after this sequence of rolls?

b. Draw the shape in its location after the following sequence of rolls: 1, 6, 4, 2. What are the new coordinates of a general point (x, y) on the shape after this sequence of rolls?

c. What sequence of rolls will produce a final image whose coordinates are all negative?

5. Describe two different sets of transformations that would move square *PQRS* onto square *WXYZ*.

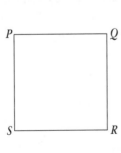
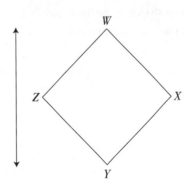

In 6–11, refer to the grid below.

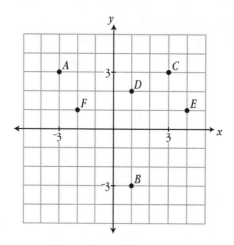

6. What are the coordinates of the image of point *A* under a translation that moves point (1, 2) onto point (‾2, 0)?

7. What are the coordinates of the image of point *B* under a translation that moves point (1, 2) onto point (4, ‾4)?

8. What are the coordinates of the image of point *C* under a translation that moves point (1, 2) onto point (‾3, ‾2)?

9. What are the coordinates of the image of point *D* under a reflection over the *x*-axis?

10. What are the coordinates of the image of point *E* under a reflection over the *y*-axis?

11. What are the coordinates of the image of point *F* under a reflection over the line *y* = *x*?

12. Identify two congruent shapes in the figure below, and explain how you could use symmetry transformations to move one shape onto the other.

In 13 and 14, refer to the grid at right.

13. Describe how you could move shape 1 to exactly match shape 1′ by using at least one translation and at least one reflection.

14. Describe how you could move shape 2 to exactly match shape 2′ by using at least one translation and at least one reflection.

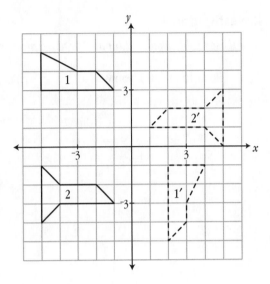

In 15–17, refer to the grid below.

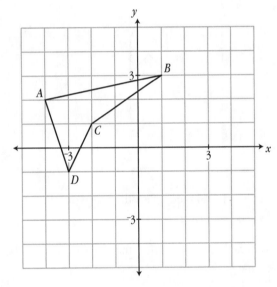

15. **a.** Draw the final image created by rotating polygon *ABCD* 90° about the origin and then reflecting the image over the *x*-axis.

   b. Draw the final image created by reflecting polygon *ABCD* over the *x*-axis and then rotating the image 90° about the origin.

   c. Are the final images in parts a and b the same? Why or why not?

16. What single transformation is equivalent to a rotation of 90° about the origin followed by a rotation of 270° about the origin?

17. What single transformation is equivalent to a reflection over the *y*-axis, followed by a reflection over the *x*-axis, followed by a reflection over the *y*-axis?

Investigation 4

Use these problems for additional practice after Investigation 4.

1. Refer to the grid below.

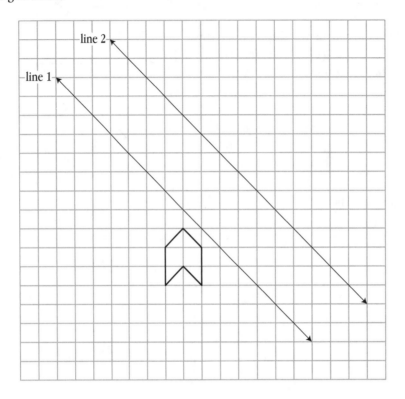

a. Reflect the shape over line 1, and then reflect the image over line 2. Describe a single transformation that would give the same final image.

b. Reflect the shape over line 2, and then reflect the image over line 1. Describe a single transformation that would give the same final image.

c. Is reflecting figures over parallel lines a commutative operation? Explain your answer.

2. Describe all the symmetry transformations for rhombus *ABCD*. Then make a table showing the results of all possible combinations of two transformations.

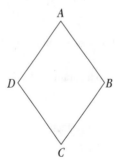

3. Shakaya has developed a system for combining pairs of letters in the set {a, b, c, d}. She uses a ♥ symbol to represent her combining operation. She made the table below to show the result of each combination of letters.

♥	a	b	c	d
a	b	c	d	a
b	c	d	a	b
c	d	a	b	c
d	a	b	c	d

a. Is Shakaya's operation commutative? Explain.

b. What is the identity element?

c. For each letter, give the inverse and explain how you know it is the inverse.

d. Evaluate each expression.

   i. (b ♥ c) ♥ a

   ii. (a ♥ b) ♥ (b ♥ c)

Blackline Masters

and Additional Practice

for *Samples and Populations*

Peanut Butter Comparisons

	Brand	Quality rating	Sodium per serving (mg)	Price per serving	Regular/ natural	Creamy/ chunky	Salted/ unsalted	Name brand/ store brand
1.	Smucker's Natural	71	15	27¢	natural	creamy	unsalted	name
2.	Deaf Smith Arrowhead Mills	69	0	32	natural	creamy	unsalted	name
3.	Adams 100% Natural	60	0	26	natural	creamy	unsalted	name
4.	Adams	60	168	26	natural	creamy	salted	name
5.	Laura Scudder's All Natural	57	165	26	natural	creamy	salted	name
6.	Country Pure Brand (Safeway)	52	225	21	natural	creamy	salted	store
7.	Hollywood Natural	34	15	32	natural	creamy	unsalted	name
8.	Smucker's Natural	89	15	27	natural	chunky	unsalted	name
9.	Adams 100% Natural	69	0	26	natural	chunky	unsalted	name
10.	Deaf Smith Arrowhead Mills	69	0	32	natural	chunky	unsalted	name
11.	Country Pure Brand (Safeway)	67	105	21	natural	chunky	salted	store
12.	Laura Scudder's All Natural	63	165	24	natural	chunky	salted	name
13.	Smucker's Natural	57	188	26	natural	chunky	salted	name
14.	Health Valley 100% Natural	40	3	34	natural	chunky	unsalted	name
15.	Jif	76	220	22	regular	creamy	salted	name
16.	Skippy	60	225	19	regular	creamy	salted	name
17.	Kroger	54	240	14	regular	creamy	salted	store
18.	NuMade (Safeway)	43	187	20	regular	creamy	salted	store
19.	Peter Pan	40	225	21	regular	creamy	salted	name
20.	Peter Pan	35	3	22	regular	creamy	unsalted	name
21.	A & P	34	225	12	regular	creamy	salted	store
22.	Food Club	33	225	17	regular	creamy	salted	store
23.	Pathmark	31	255	9	regular	creamy	salted	store
24.	Lady Lee (Lucky Stores)	23	225	16	regular	creamy	salted	store
25.	Albertsons	23	225	17	regular	creamy	salted	store
26.	Shur Fine (Shurfine Central)	11	225	16	regular	creamy	salted	store
27.	Jif	83	162	23	regular	chunky	salted	name
28.	Skippy	83	211	21	regular	chunky	salted	name
29.	Food Club	54	195	17	regular	chunky	salted	store
30.	Kroger	49	255	14	regular	chunky	salted	store
31.	A & P	46	225	11	regular	chunky	salted	store
32.	Peter Pan	45	180	22	regular	chunky	salted	name
33.	NuMade (Safeway)	40	208	21	regular	chunky	salted	store
34.	Lady Lee (Lucky Stores)	34	225	16	regular	chunky	salted	store
35.	Albertsons	31	225	17	regular	chunky	salted	store
36.	Pathmark	29	210	9	regular	chunky	salted	store
37.	Shur Fine (Shurfine Central)	26	195	16	regular	chunky	salted	store

Sources: "The Nuttiest Peanut Butter." *Consumer Reports* (September 1990): pp. 588–591.
A. J. Rossman, *Workshop Statistics: Student Activity Guide.* Carlisle, Penn.: Dickinson College, 1994, pp. 5–18.

ACE Question 9

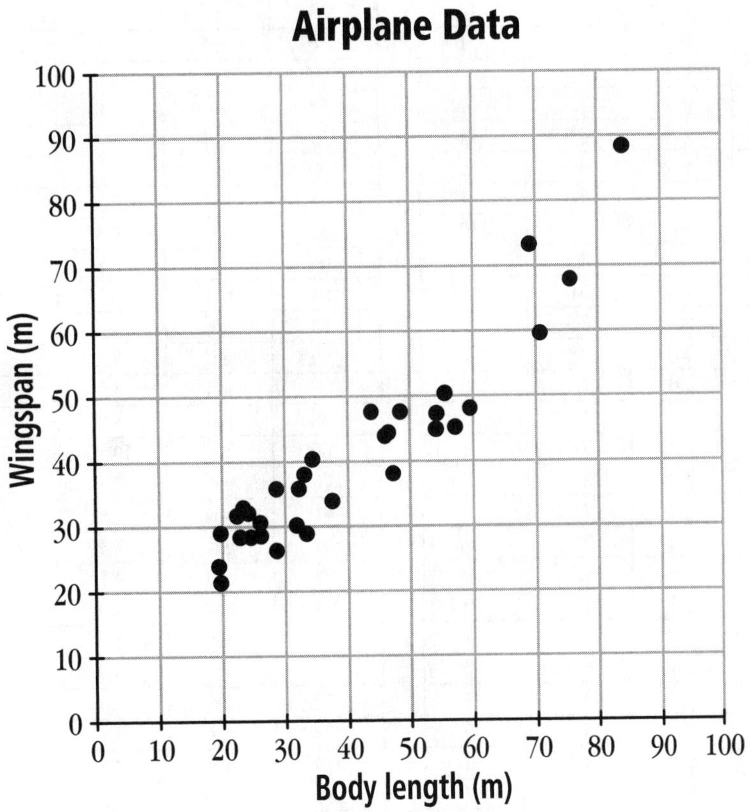
Airplane Data
Wingspan (m)
100
90
80
70
60
50
40
30
20
10
0
0
10
20
30
40
50
60
70
80
90
100
Body length (m)

Grade 8 Database

Student number	Gender	Sleep (hours)	Movies
01	boy	11.5	14
02	boy	2.0	8
03	girl	7.7	3
04	boy	9.3	1
05	boy	7.1	16
06	boy	7.5	1
07	boy	8.0	4
08	girl	7.8	1
09	girl	8.0	13
10	girl	8.0	15
11	boy	9.0	1
12	boy	9.2	10
13	boy	8.5	5
14	girl	6.0	15
15	boy	6.5	10
16	boy	8.3	2
17	girl	7.4	2
18	boy	11.2	3
19	girl	7.3	1
20	boy	8.0	0
21	girl	7.8	1
22	girl	7.8	1
23	boy	9.2	2
24	girl	7.5	0
25	boy	8.8	1
26	girl	8.5	0
27	girl	9.0	0
28	girl	8.5	0
29	boy	8.2	2
30	girl	7.8	2
31	girl	8.0	2
32	girl	7.3	8
33	boy	6.0	5
34	girl	7.5	5
35	boy	6.5	5
36	boy	9.3	1
37	girl	8.2	3
38	boy	7.3	3
39	girl	7.4	6
40	girl	8.5	7
41	boy	5.5	17
42	boy	6.5	3
43	boy	7.0	5
44	girl	8.5	2
45	girl	9.3	4
46	girl	8.0	15
47	boy	8.5	10
48	girl	6.2	11
49	girl	11.8	10
50	girl	9.0	4

Student number	Gender	Sleep (hours)	Movies
51	boy	5.0	4
52	boy	6.5	5
53	girl	8.5	2
54	boy	9.1	15
55	girl	7.5	2
56	girl	8.5	1
57	girl	8.0	2
58	girl	7.0	7
59	girl	8.4	10
60	girl	9.5	1
61	girl	7.3	5
62	girl	7.3	4
63	boy	8.5	3
64	boy	9.0	3
65	boy	9.0	4
66	girl	7.3	5
67	girl	5.7	0
68	girl	5.5	0
69	boy	10.5	7
70	girl	7.5	1
71	boy	7.8	0
72	girl	7.3	1
73	boy	9.3	2
74	boy	9.0	1
75	boy	8.7	1
76	boy	8.5	3
77	girl	9.0	1
78	boy	8.0	1
79	boy	8.0	4
80	boy	6.5	0
81	boy	8.0	0
82	girl	9.0	8
83	girl	8.0	0
84	boy	7.0	0
85	boy	9.0	6
86	boy	7.3	0
87	girl	9.0	3
88	girl	7.5	5
89	boy	8.0	0
90	girl	7.5	6
91	boy	8.0	4
92	boy	9.0	4
93	boy	7.0	0
94	boy	8.0	3
95	boy	8.3	3
96	boy	8.3	14
97	girl	7.8	5
98	girl	8.5	1
99	girl	8.3	3
100	boy	7.5	2

Box-Plot Template for Grade 8 Database

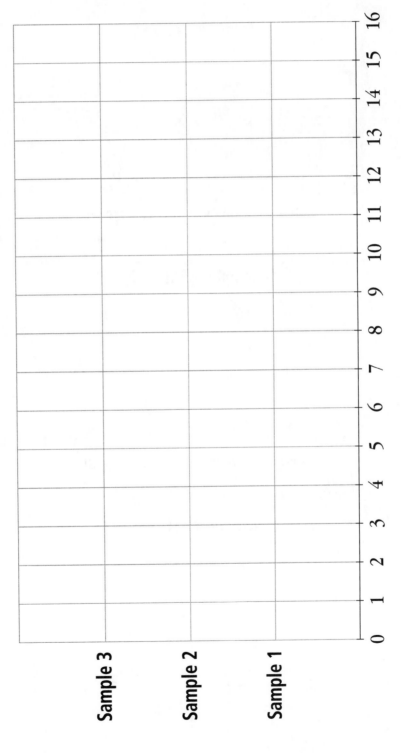

Line-Plot Template for Movie Values

Samples of Size 5

```
0.0   0.5   1.0   1.5   2.0   2.5   3.0   3.5   4.0   4.5   5.0   5.5   6.0   6.5   7.0
```
Median number of movies watched

Samples of Size 10

```
0.0   0.5   1.0   1.5   2.0   2.5   3.0   3.5   4.0   4.5   5.0   5.5   6.0   6.5   7.0
```
Median number of movies watched

Samples of Size 25

```
0.0   0.5   1.0   1.5   2.0   2.5   3.0   3.5   4.0   4.5   5.0   5.5   6.0   6.5   7.0
```
Median number of movies watched

Field A

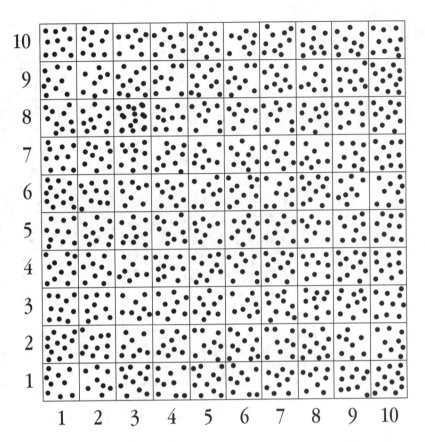

Field B

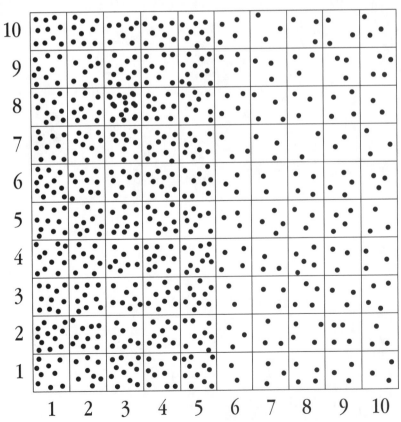

Field C

Apply some of the data analysis techniques you learned in earlier statistics work to compare the quality ratings for natural brands and regular brands.

In general, do natural brands or regular brands have higher quality ratings? Use the results of your analysis to justify your choice.

Quality Ratings for Regular Brands

Stem plot   Rotated stem plot

```
0|
1| 1
2| 3 3 6 9
3| 1 1 3 4 4 5
4| 0 0 3 5 6 9
5| 4 4
6| 0
7| 6
8| 3 3
9|
```

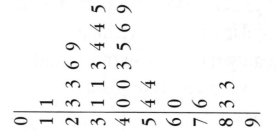

Key

2 | 6 means 26

Transforming a Rotated Stem Plot into a Histogram

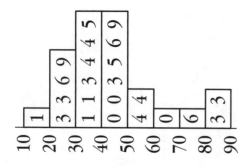

Quality Ratings for Natural and Regular Brands

Natural brands   Regular brands

```
          | 0 |
          | 1 | 1
          | 2 | 3 3 6 9
        4 | 3 | 1 1 3 4 4 5
        0 | 4 | 0 0 3 5 6 9
    7 7 2 | 5 | 4 4
9 9 9 7 3 0 0 | 6 | 0
          1 | 7 | 6
          9 | 8 | 3 3
          | 9 |
```

Quality Ratings for Natural Brands

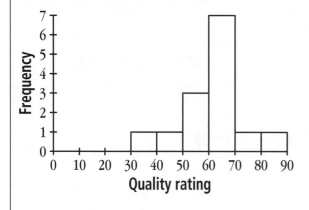

Quality Ratings for Regular Brands

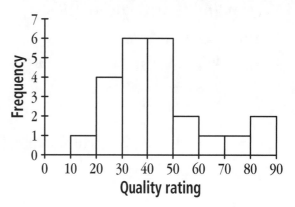

To construct a box plot showing the distribution of quality ratings for the natural brands of peanut butter, first order the data and find the five-number summary. Then, draw the number line and make the box plot.

Natural brand	Quality rating	Five-number summary
Hollywood Natural	34	← minimum = 34
Health Valley 100% Natural	40	
Country Pure Brand (Safeway)	52	
Laura Scudder's All Natural	57	← lower quartile = 57
Smucker's Natural	57	
Adams 100% Natural	60	
Adams	60	← median = 61.5
Laura Scudder's All Natural	63	
Country Pure Brand (Safeway)	67	
Deaf Smith Arrowhead Mills	69	
Adams 100% Natural	69	← upper quartile = 69
Deaf Smith Arrowhead Mills	69	
Smucker's Natural	71	
Smucker's Natural	89	← maximum = 89

Quality Ratings for Natural Brands

Quality rating

A. About what percent of the values in a data set are below the median? About what percent of the values in a data set are above the median?

B. The lower quartile, median, and upper quartile divide a data distribution into four parts. These four parts are called the *first, second, third,* and *fourth quartiles* of the distribution.

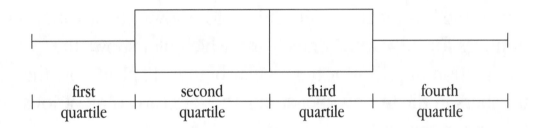

first quartile   second quartile   third quartile   fourth quartile

About what percent of the values in a data distribution are in each quartile?

C. Use the box plots of quality ratings for regular and natural brands to help you decide which type of peanut butter—regular or natural—is of higher quality. Explain your reasoning.

A. Calculate the five-number summary for the prices of the natural brands.

B. Calculate the five-number summary for the prices of the regular brands.

C. Compare the five-number summaries you found in parts A and B with the box plots. Decide which plot shows the distribution of prices for the natural brands and which plot shows the distribution of prices for the regular brands. Explain how the numbers in the five-number summaries are shown by various features of the plots.

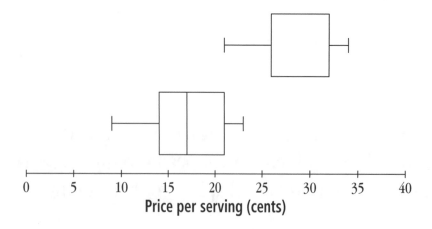

Peanut Butter Prices

Price per serving (cents)

D. How do the prices of the natural brands compare with the prices of the regular brands? Explain how you can make this comparison by using the box plots.

E. If *price* were the only factor a buyer considered, would natural peanut butter or regular peanut butter be a better choice?

If *quality* were the only factor a buyer considered, would natural peanut butter or regular peanut butter be a better choice? Explain your reasoning.

Justify your answers to the questions below with statistics and box plots.

A. Compare the quality ratings of the creamy brands with the quality ratings of the chunky brands. Based on quality, are creamy brands or chunky brands a better choice?

B. Compare the quality ratings of the salted brands with the quality ratings of the unsalted brands. Based on quality, are salted brands or unsalted brands a better choice?

C. Compare the quality ratings of the name brands with the quality ratings of the store brands. Based on quality, are name brands or store brands a better choice?

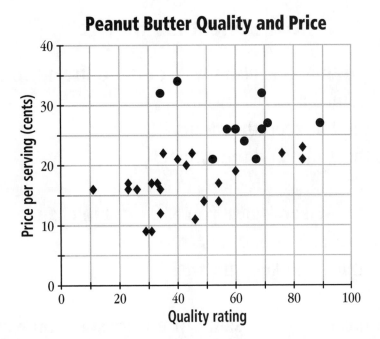

Peanut Butter Quality and Price

A. Which plot symbol, ● or ◆, represents data for natural peanut butter? Which represents data for regular peanut butter?

B. Is there an overall relationship between quality and price? Explain.

C. Do any (quality rating, price) data pairs appear to be unusual? Explain your reasoning.

D. 1. How can you use the scatter plot to compare the quality ratings of the natural brands with the quality ratings of the regular brands?

2. How can you use the scatter plot to compare the prices of the natural brands with the prices of the regular brands?

How Honest Is America?

A. If you found someone else's wallet on the street, would you
    1. try to return it to the owner?
    2. return it, but keep the money?
    3. keep the wallet and the money?

B. If a cashier mistakenly gave you $10 extra in change, would you
    1. tell the cashier about the error?
    2. say nothing and keep the cash?

C. Would you cheat on an exam if you were sure you wouldn't get caught?
    1. yes
    2. no

D. If you found someone else's telephone calling card, would you use it?
    1. yes
    2. no

E. Do you feel that you are an honest person in most situations?
    1. yes
    2. no

Call 1-900-555-8281, and enter your answers by pressing the appropriate number keys.

A. A *sampling plan* is a strategy for choosing a sample from a population. What is the sampling plan for this survey? What are the population and the sample for this survey?

B. Suppose 5280 people answered the survey, and 4224 of them pressed 2 for question C. What percent of the callers said they would not cheat on an exam?

C. Of the 5280 callers, 1584 pressed 1 for question D. What percent of the callers said they would not use someone else's calling card?

D. The U.S. population is about 260 million. Based on the results of this survey, how many people in the United States would not cheat on an exam? How many would not use someone else's calling card?

E. List some reasons why predictions about all Americans based on this survey might be inaccurate.

Ms. Baker's class wants to find out how many students in their school wear braces on their teeth. The class divides into four groups. Each group devises a plan for sampling the school population.

- Each member of group 1 will survey the students who ride on his or her school bus.

- Group 2 will survey every fourth person in the cafeteria line.

- Group 3 will read a notice on the school's morning announcements asking for volunteers for their survey.

- Group 4 will randomly select 30 students for their survey from a list of three-digit student ID numbers. They will roll a 10-sided number cube three times to generate each number.

A. What are the advantages and disadvantages of each sampling plan?

B. Which plan do you think would most accurately predict the number of students in the school who wear braces? That is, which plan do you think will give the most *representative* sample? Explain your answer.

In this problem, you will work with a partner to design a survey to gather information about middle school and high school students and their plans for the future. Your survey should include questions about characteristics of the students, such as age, gender, and favorite school subject. Your survey should also gather information about what students plan to do after graduation from high school.

For example, your survey might include questions about the following topics:

- Students' plans for college or a job immediately after high school
- The types of careers students would like to pursue
- The places students would like to live

A. Work with a partner to develop a first draft of a survey. Exchange surveys with another pair of students, and critique each other's surveys.

B. Prepare a final version of your survey.

C. Write a paragraph describing a sampling plan you could use to survey students in your school.

Imagine that you have two tickets to a sold-out rock concert, and your six best friends all want to go with you. To choose a friend to attend the concert, you want to use a strategy that gives each friend an equally likely chance of being selected. Which of the strategies below would accomplish this? Explain your reasoning.

Strategy 1: The first person who calls you on the phone tonight gets to go with you.

Strategy 2: You assign each friend a different whole number from 1 to 6. Then, you roll a six-sided number cube. The number that is rolled determines who attends the concert.

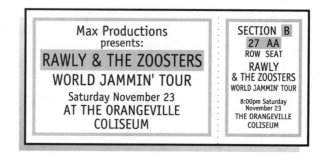

Strategy 3: You tell each friend to meet you by the rear door right after school. You toss a coin to choose between the first two friends who arrive.

© Prentice-Hall, Inc.

In this problem, each member of your group will select a random sample of students and calculate the five-number summary for the movie data. Use spinners, 10-sided number cubes, a graphing calculator, or some other method to select your sample.

A. Select a random sample of 25 students. For each student in your sample, record the number of movies watched. (Each sample should contain 25 *different* students, so if you select a student who is already in the sample, select another.)

B. Calculate the five-number summary for the movie data for your sample.

C. With your group, make box plots of the movie data for your group's samples on Labsheet 3.2.

D. What can you conclude about the movie-viewing behavior of the population of 100 students based on the patterns in the samples selected by your group? Explain how you used the data from your samples to arrive at your conclusions.

E. Compare your findings with those of other groups in your class. Describe the similarities and differences you find.

A. In Problem 3.2, you calculated five-number summaries for the movie data for random samples of 25 students. Work with your class to make a line plot of the medians found by all groups. Compare these results with the median for the population of 100 students.

B. 1. Select three random samples of 5 students, and find the median movie value for each sample. Compare the medians for your samples with the population median.

2. Compare the medians for your samples with the medians found by other members of your group. Describe the similarities or differences you find.

3. Record the medians found by your group on the board. When all groups have recorded their medians, make a line plot of the medians.

C. 1. Select three random samples of 10 students, and find the median movie value for each sample. Compare the medians for your samples with the population median.

2. Compare the medians for your samples with the medians found by other members of your group. Describe the similarities or differences you find.

3. Record the medians found by your group on the board. When all groups have recorded their medians, make a line plot of the medians.

D. Compare the distribution of medians for samples of size 5, 10, and 25. Write a paragraph describing how the median estimates for samples of different sizes compare with the actual population median.

Samples of Size 5

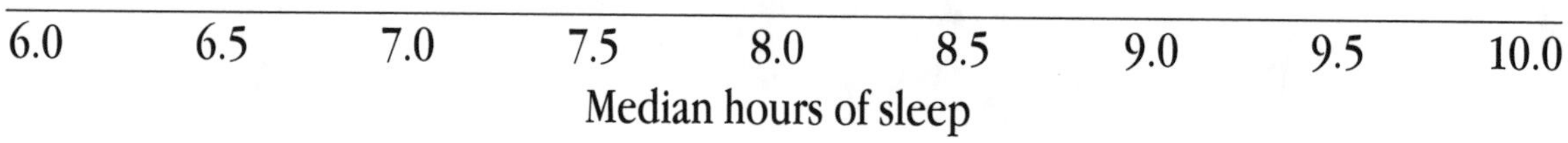

| 6.0 | 6.5 | 7.0 | 7.5 | 8.0 | 8.5 | 9.0 | 9.5 | 10.0 |

Median hours of sleep

Samples of Size 10

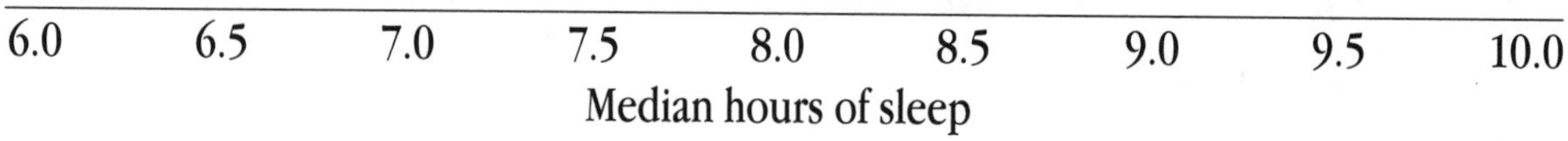

| 6.0 | 6.5 | 7.0 | 7.5 | 8.0 | 8.5 | 9.0 | 9.5 | 10.0 |

Median hours of sleep

Samples of Size 25

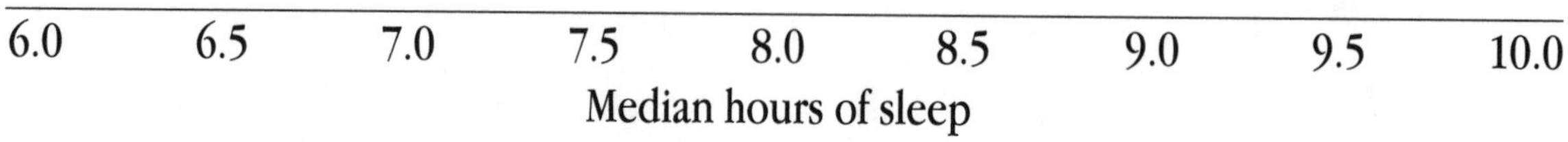

| 6.0 | 6.5 | 7.0 | 7.5 | 8.0 | 8.5 | 9.0 | 9.5 | 10.0 |

Median hours of sleep

The archaeologists hypothesized that Native Americans inhabiting the same area of the country during the same time period would have fashioned similar tools.

A. Use what you know about statistics and data representations to compare the lengths of the arrowheads discovered at the new sites with the lengths of the arrowheads from the known sites. Based on your comparisons, during which time period— 4000 B.C. to A.D. 500 or A.D. 500 to A.D. 1600—do you think site I was settled? During which time period do you think site II was settled? Explain how your statistics and graphs support your answers.

B. Compare the widths of the arrowheads discovered at the new sites with the widths of the arrowheads from the known sites. Do your findings support your answers from part A? Explain.

C. If the archaeologists had collected only a few arrowheads from each new site, might they have reached a different conclusion? Explain your answer.

A. Conduct the simulation Ted describes. You might use a chart like this to tally the number of chips in each cookie.

cookie 1 _____

cookie 2 _____

cookie 3 _____

cookie 4 _____

cookie 5 _____

cookie 6 _____

cookie 7 _____

cookie 8 _____

cookie 9 _____

cookie 10 _____

cookie 11 _____

cookie 12 _____

Generate random numbers until each cookie contains at least five chips. When you are finished, find the total number of chips in the entire batch.

B. Your teacher will display the stem values for a stem plot. Add your number-of-chips data to the plot.

C. Jeff and Ted want to be quite certain there will be at least five chips in each cookie, but they don't want to waste money by mixing in too many chocolate chips. Based on your class data, how many chips would you advise Jeff and Ted to use in each batch? Explain your answer.

Dear Family,

The next unit in your child's mathematics class this year is *Samples and Populations.* The unit will involve your child in the process of statistical investigation. As part of this process, we will pay special attention to the ways that data are collected.

The U.S. census attempts to gather information from every household in the United States. However, in most studies of large populations, data are gathered from a *sample,* or portion, of the population. The data from the sample are then used to make predictions or draw conclusions about the population. This technique is often used, for example, by pollsters during elections.

In this unit, students will explore ways to compare sets of data by examining a national magazine's study about the quality of many brands of peanut butter. Don't be surprised if your child comes home with some recommendations for new kinds of peanut butter to try!

Students will then explore what it means to look at only a sample of a population and will think about how to design and distribute surveys. They will also explore sample size and the ways in which samples can be selected.

Here are some strategies for helping your child during this unit:

- Talk with your child about the situations presented in the unit.

- Using newspapers, magazines, television, or radio, help your child identify situations in which statistics are being used, paying particular attention to who or what was sampled.

- Talk about whether data from a particular study can be used to make accurate predictions about a larger population.

- Review your child's notebook and ask for explanations of the work.

- Encourage your child's efforts in completing homework assignments.

If you have any questions or suggestions about your child's mathematics program, please feel free to call.

Sincerely,

Estimada familia,

La próxima unidad del programa de matemáticas de su hijo o hija para este curso se llama *Samples and Populations* (Muestras y poblaciones). A través de ella su hijo o hija participará en el proceso de las investigaciones estadísticas. Y como parte de dicho proceso, prestaremos una especial atención a las diferentes maneras de recoger datos.

El censo de los Estados Unidos intenta reunir datos sobre todas y cada una de las familias que viven en este país. Sin embargo, en la mayoría de los estudios realizados sobre grandes poblaciones, los datos se recogen de una *muestra,* es decir, de una parte de los habitantes. Una vez recogidos, esos datos se utilizan para hacer predicciones o para sacar conclusiones sobre la población. Así, por ejemplo, esta técnica se emplea frecuentemente en las encuestas electorales.

En esta unidad los alumnos explorarán diversas maneras de comparar conjuntos de datos; al respecto, examinarán un estudio realizado por una revista estadounidense que trata sobre la calidad de numerosas marcas de mantequilla de maní. ¡No les extrañe que su hijo o hija les recomiende que prueben algún nuevo tipo de mantequilla de maní!

Más adelante, los alumnos explorarán lo que supone examinar sólo una muestra de la población y pensarán sobre el diseño y la distribución de las encuestas. Además, investigarán el tamaño de las muestras y las formas en que éstas pueden ser seleccionadas.

Aparecen a continuación algunas estrategias que ustedes pueden emplear para ayudar a su hijo o hija durante el estudio de esta unidad:

- Hablen con él o ella sobre las situaciones presentadas en la unidad.

- Empleen los periódicos, las revistas, la televisión o la radio para ayudarle a identificar situaciones en las que se utilicen las estadísticas; para ello, presten una especial atención tanto a las personas como a los objetos que constituyen las muestras.

- Decidan juntos si los datos de un estudio determinado pueden usarse para hacer predicciones precisas sobre una población mayor.

- Repasen su cuaderno y pídanle que les explique su trabajo.

- Anímenle a esforzarse para que complete la tarea.

Si tienen alguna pregunta o recomendación relacionada con el programa de matemáticas de su hijo o hija, no duden en llamarnos.

Atentamente,

10-Section Spinners

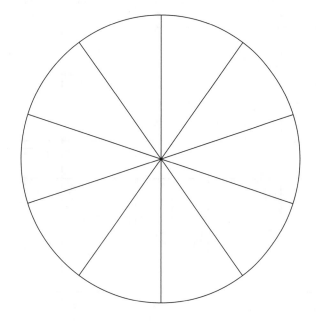
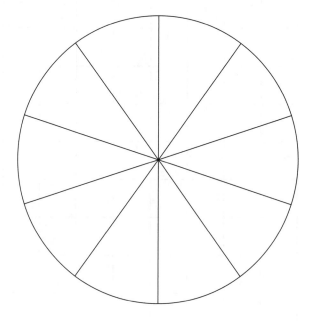
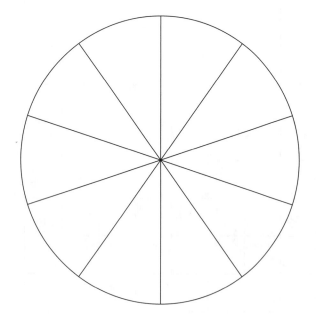
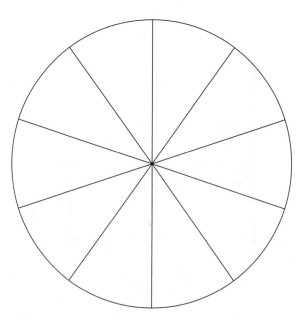

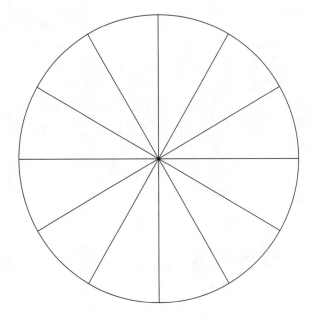

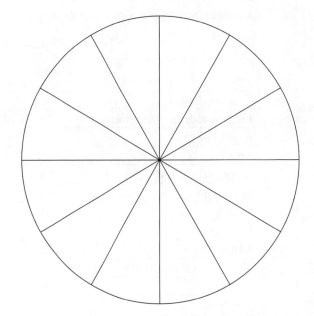

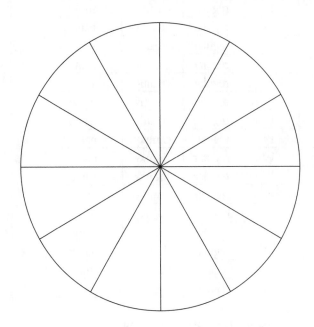

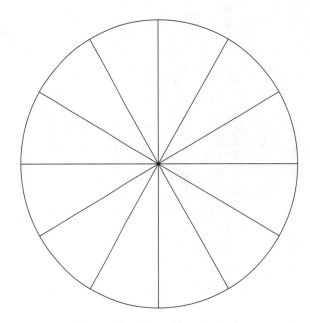

Investigation 1

Use these problems for additional practice after Investigation 1.

Another peanut butter survey was conducted more recently than the survey you studied in Investigation 1. The data for natural and regular brands are presented in the table.

Peanut Butter Comparisons

Brand	Quality rating	Sodium per serving (mg)	Price per serving	Regular/ natural	Creamy/ chunky	Name brand/ store brand
Arrowhead Mills	85	0	36	natural	creamy	name
Laura Scudder's (Southeast)	79	165	25	natural	creamy	name
Adams (West)	73	173	23	natural	creamy	name
Smucker's	73	180	26	natural	creamy	name
Nature's Cupboard (Safeway)	68	240	26	natural	creamy	store
Laura Scudder's Nutty (Southeast)	84	165	26	natural	chunky	name
Arrowhead Mills	83	0	37	natural	chunky	name
Smucker's	79	180	26	natural	chunky	name
Adams (West)	75	135	23	natural	chunky	name
Nature's Cupboard (Safeway)	72	195	26	natural	chunky	store
Jif	85	225	19¢	regular	creamy	name
Simply Jif	85	98	19	regular	creamy	name
Peter Pan	82	225	17	regular	creamy	name
Skippy	82	225	18	regular	creamy	name
Kroger	79	195	15	regular	creamy	store
Skippy Roasted Honey Nut	79	180	19	regular	creamy	name
America's Choice	77	225	17	regular	creamy	store
Reese's	68	173	19	regular	creamy	name
Townhouse (Safeway)	68	240	18	regular	creamy	store
Peter Pan Very Low Sodium	57	15	18	regular	creamy	name
Peter Pan Whipped	49	173	17	regular	creamy	name
Jif Extra Crunchy	88	195	19	regular	chunky	name
Skippy Super Chunk	87	210	19	regular	chunky	name
Peter Pan Extra Crunchy	86	180	17	regular	chunky	name
Reese's	86	120	19	regular	chunky	name
Skippy Roasted Honey Nut	86	180	19	regular	chunky	name
Kroger	84	195	15	regular	chunky	store
Simply Jif Extra Crunchy	83	75	19	regular	chunky	name
America's Choice Krunchy	80	188	17	regular	chunky	store
Townhouse (Safeway)	72	195	18	regular	chunky	store

Source: "Peanut Butter: It's Not Just for Kids Anymore." *Consumer Reports* (September 1995): pp. 576–579.

© Prentice-Hall, Inc.

1. The box plots below show the quality ratings of natural versus regular brands, creamy versus chunky brands, and name brands versus store brands. Based on these box plots, what characteristics would you look for if you wanted to choose a peanut butter based on quality rating? Explain your reasoning using the information shown in the box plots.

Quality Comparisons

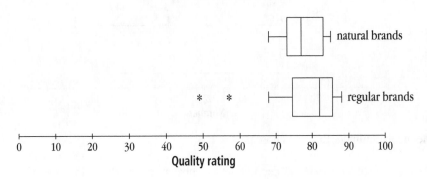

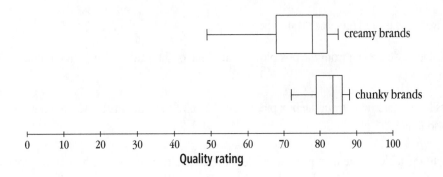

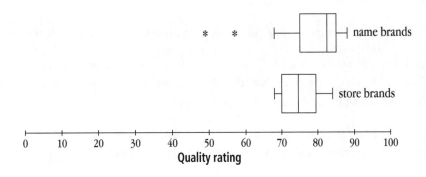

2. Make box plots to compare the peanut butters based on price. Mark any outliers with an asterisk (*). Which characteristic(s) help identify low-price peanut butters? Explain your reasoning.

Use this information in 3–8: Ms. Humphrey asked each of the 21 students in her mathematics class to choose a number between 1 and 50. Ms. Humphrey recorded the data and made this box plot:

Ms. Humphrey's Class Data

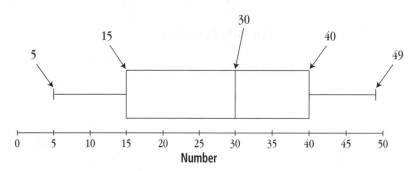

3. What is the median number that was chosen?

4. What percentage of students in Ms. Humphrey's class chose numbers above 15? Explain your reasoning.

5. About how many students chose numbers between 30 and 40? Explain your reasoning.

6. What were the least and the greatest numbers chosen?

7. Is it possible to determine from the box plot whether one of the students chose the number 27? Explain your reasoning.

8. Is it possible to determine from the box plot whether one of the students chose the number 4? Explain your reasoning.

In 9–12, refer to the table on the next page, which lists the engine type, body length, and wingspan of several airplanes flown by major airlines. The fifth column shows the ratio of wingspan to body length.

9. Finish computing the values for the fifth column.

10. What does it mean when the ratio of wingspan to body length is 1? Greater than 1? Less than 1?

11. Compute the five-number summary for jet planes and the five-number summary for propeller planes of the ratio of wingspan to body length. Explain what the medians tell you about the relationship between wingspan and body length for jet planes and for propeller planes.

12. Make box plots from your five-number summaries. Explain what your plots reveal about how jet planes and propeller planes compare based on ratio of wingspan to body length.

Airplane Data

Plane	Engine type	Body length (m)	Wingspan (m)	Wingspan-to-length ratio
Boeing 707	jet	46.6	44.4	0.953
Boeing 747	jet	70.7	59.6	0.843
Ilyushin IL-86	jet	59.5	48.1	
McDonnell Douglas DC-8	jet	57.1	45.2	
Antonov An-124	jet	69.1	73.3	
British Aerospace 146	jet	28.6	26.3	
Lockheed C-5 Galaxy	jet	75.5	67.9	
Antonov An-225	jet	84.0	88.4	
Airbus A300	jet	54.1	44.9	
Airbus A310	jet	46.0	43.9	
Airbus A320	jet	37.5	33.9	
Boeing 737	jet	33.4	28.9	
Boeing 757	jet	47.3	38.1	
Boeing 767	jet	48.5	47.6	
Lockheed Tristar L-1011	jet	54.2	47.3	
McDonnell Douglas DC-10	jet	55.5	50.4	
Aero/Boeing Spacelines Guppy	propeller	43.8	47.6	
Douglas DC-4 C-54 Skymaster	propeller	28.6	35.8	
Douglas DC-6	propeller	32.2	35.8	
Lockheed L-188 Electra	propeller	31.8	30.2	
Vickers Viscount	propeller	26.1	28.6	
Antonov An-12	propeller	33.1	38.0	
de Havilland DHC Dash-7	propeller	24.5	28.4	
Lockheed C-130 Hercules/L-100	propeller	34.4	40.4	
British Aerospace 748/ATP	propeller	26.0	30.6	
Convair 240	propeller	24.1	32.1	
Curtiss C-46 Commando	propeller	23.3	32.9	
Douglas DC-3	propeller	19.7	29.0	
Grumman Gulfstream I/I-C	propeller	19.4	23.9	
Ilyushin IL-14	propeller	22.3	31.7	
Martin 4-0-4	propeller	22.8	28.4	
Saab 340	propeller	19.7	21.4	

Source: William Berk and Frank Berk. *Airport Airplanes.* Plymouth, Mich.: Plymouth Press, 1993.

In 13–15, use the tables below, which display the results of a study of 47 half-ounce boxes of two brands of raisins. The table on the left shows the number of raisins and the mass in grams for boxes of Vine Hill raisins. The table on the right shows the results for Suntime raisins.

Vine Hill Raisins

Number in box	Mass (grams)	Number in box	Mass (grams)
29	14.78	38	16.3
35	16.59	38	16.85
35	16.01	38	17.33
35	16.55	38	17.57
36	16.99	40	16.2
38	16.34	40	16.78
38	16.3	40	17.35
39	17.83	41	17.43
39	16.66	41	16.64
39	18.36	41	16.62
39	16.93	31	14.7
40	16.25	34	16.04
40	17.92	35	16.81
40	17.12	36	16.86
40	17.37	36	16.75
42	16.95	36	17.18
42	17.45	36	15.77
44	18.48	36	16.28
35	15.64	37	16.25
36	16.88	37	17.42
36	16.36	37	16.25
36	16.3	37	15.63
37	17.25	37	17.74
37	15.61		

Suntime Raisins

Number in box	Mass (grams)	Number in box	Mass (grams)
25	14.15	31	16.13
26	16.74	31	16.6
27	15.42	32	16.6
27	16.74	33	16.55
27	15.98	33	17.11
28	17.43	34	16.88
28	16.44	34	18.1
28	16.55	35	17.63
28	15.55	35	17.32
28	15.33	26	15.34
29	16.75	28	14.11
29	16.19	29	16.94
29	16.36	29	15.16
29	17.1	29	15.75
29	16.58	29	15.65
30	16.36	30	16.5
30	16.29	31	15.83
31	15.9	31	17.17
29	16.18	32	16.6
29	15.91	32	16.59
30	16.66	32	16.38
31	15.73	33	17.11
31	16.38	34	17.24
31	16.92		

13. The two scatter plots on the next page show the data from the tables. Which scatter plot shows the data for Suntime raisins? Which shows the data for Vine Hill raisins? Explain your reasoning.

14. Is this statement true or false: "Vine Hill raisins typically have more raisins in a box than do Suntime raisins." Explain your reasoning using the two graphs.

15. Is there a relationship between the number of raisins in a box and the mass in grams? Explain your reasoning.

Scatter Plot A

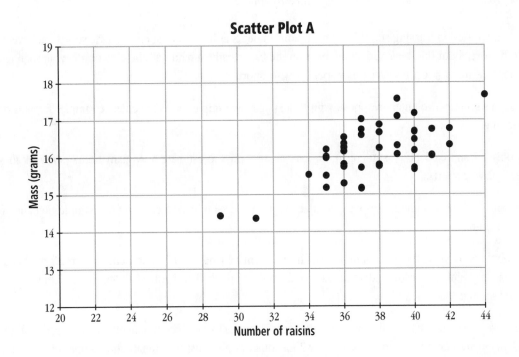

Scatter Plot B

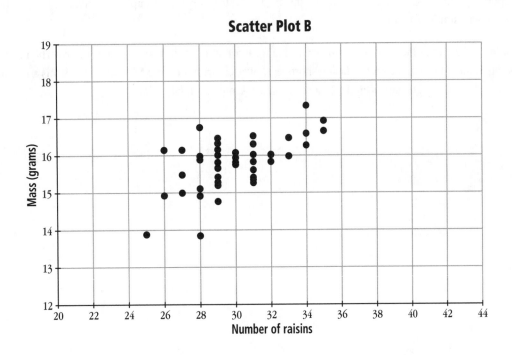

Investigation 2

Use these problems for additional practice after Investigation 2.

Aaron was interested in learning about how much time students at his school spend playing sports each week. To find out more about this, he asked all the boys on the basketball team and all the girls on the volleyball team to estimate how many hours per week they spent playing sports.

1. Is Aaron's sample a voluntary-response sample, a systematic sample, or a convenience sample? Explain your reasoning.

2. Suppose Aaron asked all the students in his mathematics class to estimate how many hours per week they spend playing sports.

   a. Would this be a voluntary-response sample, a systematic sample, or a convenience sample? Explain your reasoning.

   b. Would you expect the median number of hours spent playing sports for students in Aaron's mathematics class to be higher or lower than his sample from the basketball and volleyball teams? Explain your reasoning.

3. There are 1232 students enrolled at Aaron's school. The principal's office has an alphabetical list of all the students' names. Suppose Aaron asked every 20th student on the list to estimate the number of hours he or she spends playing sports each week. Would this be a voluntary-response sample, a systematic sample, or a convenience sample? Explain.

4. Aaron placed an ad in the school newspaper with a form for students to complete and return. The form asked how much time the student spent playing sports each week. Aaron received 53 responses. Is this a voluntary-response sample, a systematic sample, or a convenience sample? Explain.

Investigation 3

Use these problems for additional practice after Investigation 3.

In 1–4, use this information: In a survey of the cafeteria food at Metropolis Middle School, 50 students were asked to rate how well they liked the lunches on a scale of 1 to 10, with 1 being the lowest rating and 10 being the highest rating. The box plot below was made from the collected data.

Cafeteria Food Survey

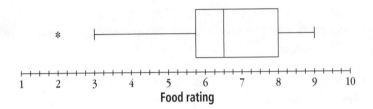

Food rating

1. What is the range of students' ratings in the sample?

2. What percent of the students in the sample rated the cafeteria food between 5.75 and 9?

3. Based on the sample data, how many of the 1000 students at Metropolis do you estimate would rate the cafeteria food 6 or higher? Explain your reasoning.

4. A rating of 8 to 10 indicates "highly satisfied" on the rating scale.

   a. What percent of students in the sample are "highly satisfied" with the cafeteria food?

   b. Estimate how many students at Metropolis Middle School would give the cafeteria food a "highly satisfied" rating.

In 5–7, use this information: Marci works on the yearbook staff at Metropolis Middle School. Of the 92 businesses in the downtown area, 41 purchased advertising space in the yearbook last year.

5. Suppose Marci wants to investigate why businesses did not advertise in the yearbook last year. Describe a sampling strategy she could use to call 10 businesses.

6. Suppose Marci wants to investigate how satisfied advertisers are with yearbook ads. Describe a sampling strategy she could use to call 10 businesses.

7. Suppose Marci wants to investigate how likely a typical downtown business is to advertise in the upcoming yearbook. Describe a sampling strategy she could use to call 10 businesses.

8. Mr. Darrow and the 29 students in his afternoon mathematics class each generated 10 random numbers between 1 and 100. Here are one student's results:

83   8   40   79   77   62   92   29   67   11

   a. Compute the five-number summary of this student's numbers and make a box plot.

   b. Select nine more samples, each containing 10 numbers between 1 and 100, using your calculator or another strategy for choosing numbers randomly. On the same scale you used in part a, make box plots for each sample.

   c. Using your box plots, about what percent of the numbers generated would you expect to fall between 29 and 79? Explain your reasoning.

9. The principal of a nearby school, Megalopolis Middle School, decided to conduct a survey of the 1107 enrolled students. She asked three teachers how many students they thought should be surveyed. One teacher said to survey 200 girls and 100 boys, the second said to randomly select and survey 50 students, and the third said to survey the first 100 students to enter the building one morning next week.

   a. Explain which of the three samples will produce data that may best represent all the students at Megalopolis.

   b. Explain why you feel that the other two samples would not be as representative of all the students as the one you chose in part a.

Investigation 4

Use these problems for additional practice after Investigation 4.

1. A group of students surveyed several pizza shops in two parts of the United States. They asked about prices and sizes of small, medium, and large cheese pizzas, and they made box plots from the data they collected.

   a. These box plots show the prices for each size pizza, including outliers. Which size appears to be the least expensive? Explain your reasoning.

   Pizza Prices

   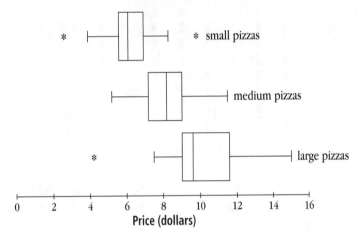

   b. One of the small pizzas had a diameter of 8 inches and a price of $3.87. Its price per square inch is $0.077. How was this calculated?

   c. These box plots show the price per square inch of pizza for each size. Which size appears to be the best buy? Explain your reasoning.

   Pizza Prices per Square Inch

   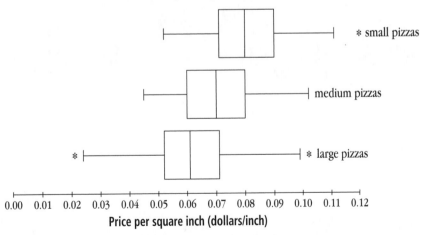

   d. Consider your responses to parts a and c. Which set of box plots better reflects the actual price of a pizza? Explain your reasoning.

2. Suppose Jeff and Ted decide to change their advertising slogan to "Seven giant chips in every cookie!" They mix 70 chips into a batch of dough and make 10 cookies from the dough. When they remove the cookies from the oven and inspect them, they count the number of chips in each cookie. Their results are shown below. Notice that only 5 of the 10 cookies contained 7 chips or more.

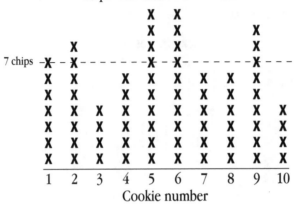

Chips in a Batch of 10 Cookies

a. Conduct a simulation to determine the number of chips needed to be added to a batch of 10 cookies until each cookie has at least 7 chips. Carry out the simulation five times so that you have five data values for the number of chips needed.

b. What is the minimum number of chips Jeff and Ted should use to be confident that each cookie will have at least 7 chips? Support your answer with statistics and graphs.

Blackline Masters

and
Additional
Practice

for
Clever Counting

Making Trains

10-car

9-car

9-car

8-car	8-car

8-car	8-car

7-car	7-car

7-car	7-car

6-car	6-car

6-car	6-car

5-car	5-car	5-car

5-car	5-car	5-car

4-car	4-car	4-car	4-car

4-car	4-car	4-car	4-car

3-car	3-car	3-car	3-car	3-car

3-car	3-car	3-car	3-car	3-car

2-car	2-car	2-car	2-car	2-car	2-car	2-car

2-car	2-car	2-car	2-car	2-car	2-car	2-car

1-car	1-car	1-car	1-car	1-car	1-car	1-car	1-car	1-car	1-car	1-car	1-car

1-car	1-car	1-car	1-car	1-car	1-car	1-car	1-car	1-car	1-car	1-car	1-car

© Prentice-Hall, Inc.

Here are the choices the artist gave the witness:

Hair	**Eyes**	**Nose**
bushy	staring	hooked
bald	beady	long and straight
	droopy	turned up
	wide open	broken

A. How many facial descriptions can you make by choosing one attribute for each feature?

B. The witness said he remembered something distinctive about the driver's mouth. The artist suggested these possibilities:

Mouth
thin and mean
toothless
sinister grin

If you consider the hair, eyes, nose, and mouth, how many facial descriptions can you make by choosing one attribute for each feature?

The witness claimed that he saw the license plate of the van. In the state in which the robbery took place, license plates contain three letters followed by three numbers. He said that it was an in-state plate containing the letters MTU.

Detective Curious wants to run each possible plate number through the computer to find out whether the registered owner has a criminal record. It takes about 20 seconds to check each plate number.

How many possible plates start with MTU?

Do you think this is a reasonable number of plates for the detective to check?

A lock sequence may have two, three, four, or five letters. A letter may not occur more than once in a sequence.

A. How many two-letter sequences are possible?

B. How many three-letter sequences are possible?

C. How many four-letter sequences are possible?

D. How many five-letter sequences are possible?

E. The security guard would not have known whether the sequence that would open Rodney's lock consisted of two, three, four, or five letters. How many possible lock sequences might she have had to try?

A. How many possible combinations are there for Rodney's lock? Assume that a number may not appear more than once in a combination.

B. How long do you think it would take someone to try all the possible combinations? Explain how you made your estimate.

A. Make a table showing the number of possible combinations for locks with from 3 to 10 marks. Consider only three-number combinations with no repeated numbers. For example, to complete the row for 3 marks, consider all possible combinations of the numbers 0, 1, and 2.

Number of marks	Number of combinations
3	
4	
5	
6	
7	
8	
9	
10	

B. Use the pattern in your table to write an equation for the relationship between the number of marks, *m*, and the number of combinations, *C*.

C. Sketch a graph of your equation for *m* values from 3 to 10.

D. How could the manager use your graph to convince the owner to buy locks with more marks?

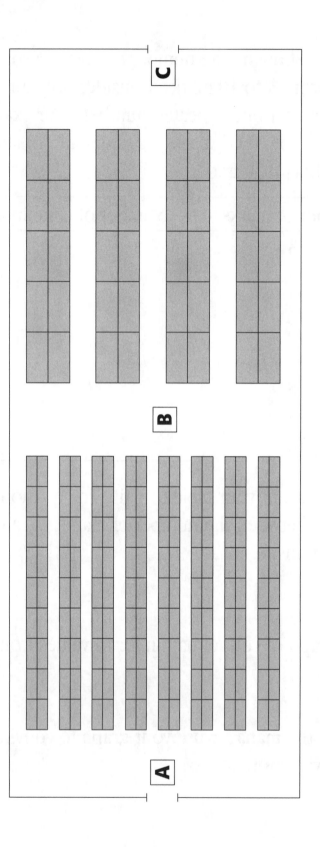

A. How many paths are there from A to B? How many paths are there from B to C?

B. How many paths are there from A to C through B? Explain your reasoning.

C. If Rodney has a small locker, how many of the paths from A to C pass by his locker?

D. If Rodney has a large locker, how many of the paths from A to C pass by his locker?

E. If Rodney has a small locker, what is the probability that the guard will *not* pass his locker on one of her rounds?

F. If Rodney has a large locker, what is the probability that the guard will *not* pass his locker on one of her rounds?

A. In this network, a single edge connects node A to node B, and 8 edges connect node B to node C. How many paths are there from node A to node C that pass through node B?

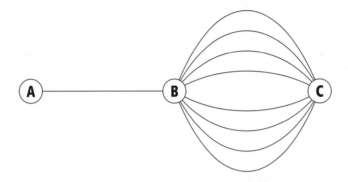

B. In this network, 2 edges connect node A to node B, and 5 edges connect node B to node C. How many paths are there from node A to node C that pass through node B?

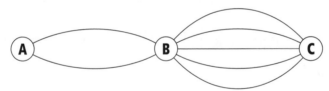

C. In another network, 25 edges connect node A to node B, and 32 edges connect node B to node C. How many paths are there from node A to node C that pass through node B? Explain your reasoning.

A. 1. Design at least three networks with nodes A, B, and C and 12 edges. Each edge should connect node A to node B or node B to node C.

2. For each network you drew, record the number of edges from node A to node B, the number of edges from node B to node C, and the total number of paths from node A to node C. Look for a pattern in your results.

3. Use your findings from part 2 to help you draw the network with the maximum number of paths from node A to node C. Explain how you know that your network has the maximum number of paths.

B. Design a network with nodes A, B, C, and D and 12 edges that has the maximum number of paths from node A to node D through nodes B and C. How did you decide how to distribute the 12 edges?

C. Suppose you are given a specific number of nodes and a specific number of edges. How can you design a network with the maximum number of paths from the first node to the last node?

D. Describe how the numbers of edges between consecutive pairs of nodes are related to the total number of paths in a network.

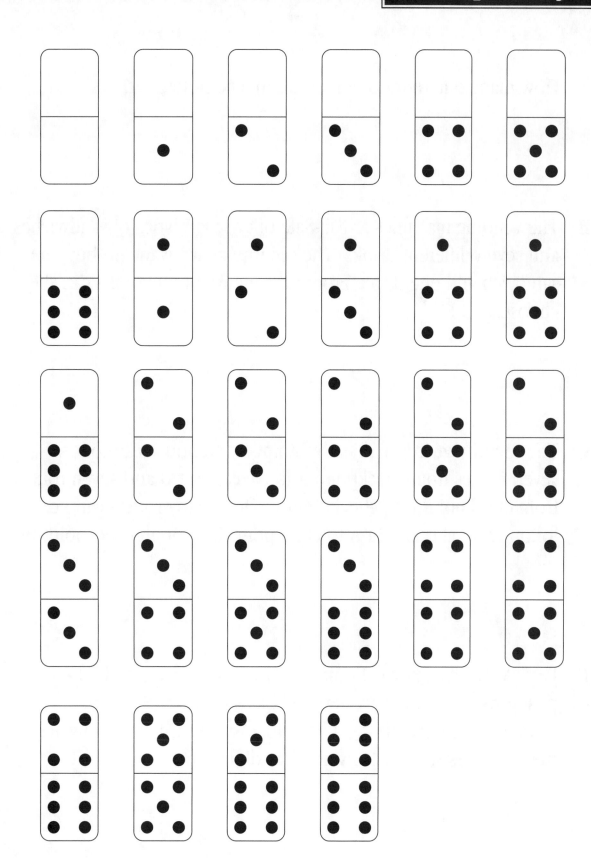

A. How many different dominoes are in a complete set?

B. The vending machines at Fail-Safe offer seven types of sandwiches and seven different drinks. The security guard wants to buy one sandwich and one drink. From how many combinations can she choose?

C. The security guard in a nearby storage warehouse can follow seven routes from checkpoint A to checkpoint B and seven routes from checkpoint B to checkpoint C. How many routes can he follow from checkpoint A to checkpoint C through checkpoint B?

D. Parts A–C each involve finding the number of ways to fill two positions when there are seven choices for each position. Compare the strategies you used to answer each part. How are the strategies similar? How are they different?

The manager narrowed his choices to six models: the ACME CrimeStopper, the BurgleProof 2000, the Citadel, the Deterrent, the EverSafe, and the Fortress. He chose two locks to bring to the meeting.

A. There are several ways the manager could have chosen the two locks. In how many different ways could the manager have chosen the two locks? Prove your answer is correct by listing all the possible pairs of locks.

B. If the manager had taken three locks to the meeting, in how many different ways could he have chosen them? Prove your answer is correct by listing all the possible sets of three locks.

C. How is finding the number of different ways the manager could have chosen the locks similar to and different from finding the number of lock combinations in Investigation 2?

You know as much as the detective does about counting combinations and calculating probabilities. Imagine that the detective asks you to help her with the case.

A. Which pieces of evidence would you investigate further? How would you proceed with your investigation?

B. What questions would you ask the security guard, the manager, or someone else involved in the case?

C. Does the evidence from the second robbery clear any of the suspects? Who are your suspects now? Why?

Dear Family,

The last unit in your child's course of study in mathematics class this year involves one of the most common aspects of arithmetic that we encountered as young children, but that can become complicated very quickly: counting.

When we learned to count, we probably memorized the numbers 1, 2, 3, and so on. Only later did we understand what those words meant. In their mathematics work this year, students have had many opportunities to further their understanding of numbers and operations. In *Clever Counting,* they learn to recognize situations in which multiplication can help them to count how many ways certain events can happen. As students work on the unit, they will increase their skill with multiplication and making sense of large numbers.

The task of counting becomes complicated when we place conditions on what we are counting. Students will investigate a fictitious robbery in this unit. In the process, they will be asked to count, among other things, the number of combinations a lock can have, the number of license plates that are possible with particular characteristics, and the number of paths a night guard might travel during periodic inspection rounds.

Here are some strategies for helping your child during this unit:

- Ask for an explanation of the ideas about counting that are presented in the book.

- Help your child locate examples of counting that people deal with in their everyday lives.

- Discuss with your child real situations in which counting techniques are used; for example, the field of cryptoanalysis, a branch of mathematics in which people work with secret codes such as those used in banks and most businesses.

- Encourage your child to do his or her homework every day. Look over the homework and make sure all questions are answered and that explanations are clear.

As always, if you have any questions or suggestions about your child's mathematics program, please feel free to call.

Sincerely,

Estimada familia,

La última unidad del programa de matemáticas de su hijo o hija para este curso trata sobre uno de los aspectos de la aritmética que cuando fuimos niños más comúnmente utilizamos y que puede llegar a complicarse con suma facilidad: el contar.

Cuando aprendimos a contar, probablemente lo hicimos memorizando los números 1, 2, 3 y así sucesivamente. Y fue en algún momento posterior cuando realmente llegamos a entender lo que significaban esas palabras. En el trabajo matemático que los alumnos han realizado este año han tenido muchas oportunidades para aumentar sus conocimientos acerca de los números y las operaciones. En *Clever Counting* (Contar inteligentemente), aprenden a identificar situaciones en las que la multiplicación les puede ayudar a contar la cantidad de maneras en que pueden ocurrir ciertos sucesos. Durante el estudio de esta unidad, perfeccionarán sus destrezas relacionadas con la multiplicación y con la comprensión de las grandes cifras.

El contar puede llegar a ser complicado cuando imponemos condiciones al objeto que contamos. En esta unidad los alumnos examinarán un robo ficticio y, como parte de dicho proceso, se les pedirá que cuenten, entre otras cosas, el número de combinaciones que puede tener una cerradura, el número de placas de matrícula que puede haber con ciertas características y el número de caminos diferentes que un guarda nocturno puede recorrer durante sus rondas periódicas de vigilancia.

Aparecen a continuación algunas estrategias que ustedes pueden emplear para ayudar a su hijo o hija en esta unidad:

- Pídanle que les explique las ideas relativas al conteo que se presentan en el libro.

- Ayúdenle a buscar ejemplos en la vida diaria en los que la gente tenga que contar.

- Comenten juntos situaciones reales en las que se emplean técnicas de conteo. Un ejemplo puede ser el campo del criptoanálisis, una rama de las matemáticas en la que se manejan códigos secretos, como los utilizados en los bancos y en la mayoría de los negocios.

- Anímenle a hacer la tarea todos los días. Repásenla para asegurarse de que conteste todas las preguntas y escriba con claridad las explicaciones.

Y como de costumbre, si ustedes tienen alguna duda o recomendación relacionada con el programa de matemáticas de su hijo o hija, no duden en llamarnos.

Atentamente,

Investigation 1

Use these problems for additional practice after Investigation 1.

Three buckets each contain four balls marked with a letter or a number.

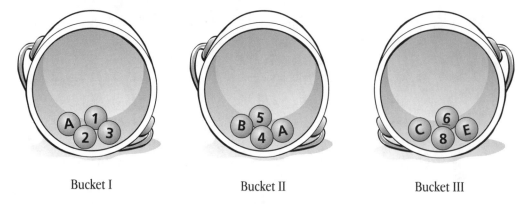

| Bucket I | Bucket II | Bucket III |

1. Suppose one ball is drawn from bucket I and one ball is drawn from bucket II. Make a counting tree to show how many different combinations of characters—letters or numbers—are possible.

2. Suppose one ball is drawn from bucket II and one ball is drawn from bucket III. How many different combinations of characters are possible? Explain your reasoning.

3. Suppose one ball is drawn from bucket I and one ball is drawn from bucket III. How many different combinations of characters are possible? Explain your reasoning.

4. Suppose one ball is drawn from each bucket. How many possible combinations contain *only* numbers? Explain your reasoning.

5. Suppose one ball is drawn from each bucket. How many possible combinations contain *only* letters? Explain your reasoning.

6. Suppose one ball is drawn from each bucket. How many possible combinations *do not* contain consonants or odd numbers? Explain your reasoning.

Use this information to answer 7–9: In one state, license plates contain three letters followed by four numbers. The letters I, O, and Q are not used because they might be mistaken for the numbers 1 or 0.

7. How many different plates could be made using this system? Explain your reasoning.

8. How many cars in this state can have plates in which all the letters are vowels (A, E, I, O, or U)? Explain your reasoning.

9. How many cars in this state can have plates in which all the digits are odd? Explain your reasoning.

10. Telephone numbers consist of a three-digit *prefix* followed by a four-digit number, such as 555-2870. Suppose the numbers 0, 1, 2, 3, 4, 5, 6, 7, 8, 9 can be used for each digit. How many local telephone numbers are possible? Explain your reasoning.

In North America, telephone numbers consist of a three-digit *area code*, followed by a three-digit *prefix*, followed by four more digits. In the telephone number (517) 555-2870, 517 is the area code. In 11–14, assume that the digits from 0 to 9 can be used in any location in a phone number.

11. In a state with 4 area codes, how many telephone numbers are possible? Explain your reasoning.

12. In a state with 12 area codes, how many telephone numbers are possible?

13. In a state with 8 area codes, how many telephone numbers are possible?

14. Suppose a state is running out of telephone numbers and anticipates the need for 10 million new telephone numbers over the next five years. How many new area codes will the state need to meet this increase? Explain your reasoning.

The Metropolis school district has an enrollment of 26,479 students. The district wants to assign an identification code to each student.

15. Suppose you are in charge of developing an ID system. Describe a system that would provide enough ID codes for all the students and require the fewest characters (letters or numbers). Explain your reasoning.

16. Suppose the ID codes cannot contain letters. Describe an ID system that would provide enough ID codes and require the fewest characters. Explain your answer.

17. Are your answers to 16 and 17 different? Explain why they are the same or different.

Investigation 2

Use these problems for additional practice after Investigation 2.

In 1–6, consider any combination of letters a "word," even if you can't pronounce the word and have no idea whether it has any meaning.

1. How many three-letter words can be made with the letters X, Y, and Z if letters *can* be repeated?

2. How many three-letter words can be made with the letters X, Y, and Z if letters *cannot* be repeated?

3. How many three-letter words can be made with the letters Q, R, X, Y, and Z if letters *can* be repeated?

4. How many three-letter words can be made with the letters Q, R, X, Y, and Z if letters *cannot* be repeated?

5. How many *three-letter* words can be made with the letters X and L with repeats allowed?

6. How many *five-letter* words can be made with the letters X and L with repeats allowed?

In 7–9, use this information: Felix and Emily are decorating the school gym for the spring dance. They decide to string balloons in a repeating pattern of four balloons. They have six different colors of balloons to choose from.

7. If the four balloons in the pattern will each be a different color, how many patterns are possible? Explain how you found your answer.

8. Suppose Felix and Emily eliminate the two colors that are the least bright. If the four balloons in the pattern will each be a different color, how many patterns are possible?

9. If Emily and Felix decide to use only four colors, but make the pattern five balloons long with one color repeated, how many patterns are possible? Explain how you found your answer.

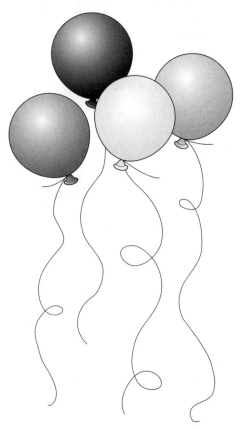

10. The science club is holding a raffle to raise money for new laboratory equipment. The raffle tickets contain four characters. The first character can be any letter of the alphabet. Each of the three remaining characters can be any number from 0 to 9. To win, a raffle ticket must match a randomly generated string exactly.

a. How many tickets are possible that begin with the letter K?

b. How many tickets are possible that end with two zeros?

c. Kathy, the treasurer of the science club, says that she has just realized that since there are 1150 students and 50 teachers at the school, it is likely that even if every student and teacher bought a raffle ticket, no one would have a winning ticket.

   i. Do you agree with Kathy? Explain why or why not.

   ii. Assuming that every raffle ticket is different, how many raffle tickets would each student and teacher have to buy to guarantee that someone would have the winning ticket? Explain your answer.

d. Based on your answer to part c, would you change the character string on the raffle tickets? If so, describe a new character string and why it would be better. If not, explain why you would leave the string unchanged.

11. In one state, license plates contain three letters followed by four numbers. The letters I, O, and Q are not used because they might be mistaken for the numbers 1 or 0. How many different plates could be made in this state if no letters or numbers can be repeated? Explain your reasoning.

12. There are eight Connected Mathematics units for grade 8.

a. In how many different sequences can the eight units be arranged on a bookshelf?

b. In how many different sequences can the eight units be arranged on a bookshelf if *Clever Counting* is the last unit in the sequence?

Investigation 3

Use these problems for additional practice after Investigation 3.

Use the network below to answer questions 1–5.

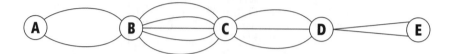

1. How many nodes does the network have?

2. How many edges does the network have?

3. How many paths are there from node B to node D?

4. How many paths are there from node B to node E?

5. How many paths are there from node A to node E?

6. **a.** The network below represents the highways connecting four cities. How many highway routes are there from city W to city Z that pass through cities X and Y?

   b. How many different highway round trips are there from city W to city Z and back to city W?

   c. Suppose one of the highways from city X to city Y is closed due to road construction. How does that change the number of highway routes from city W to city Z through cities X and Y?

7. Design a network with nodes A, B, C, and D and exactly 15 edges that has the maximum number of paths from node A to node D through nodes B and C. How many paths does your network have?

8. Design a network with nodes E, F, G, and H so that there are exactly 27 paths from node E to node H passing through nodes F and G.

9. Design a network with nodes A, B, C, D, E, and F so that there are exactly 32 paths from node A to node F passing through nodes B, C, D, and E.

10. Design a network with nodes Z, ZZ, and ZZZ so that there are exactly 3 paths from node Z to node ZZZ passing through node ZZ.

11. J, K, L, and M are the corners of a square. There is one direct path between each pair of corners. How many paths are there from J through each of the other three points and back to J? Explain.

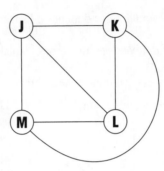

Investigation 4

Use these problems for additional practice after Investigation 4.

1. How many different dominoes are in a set of *double-three* dominoes, which have from 0 to 3 pips on each half? Explain how you found your answer.

2. How many different dominoes are in a set of *double-seven* dominoes, which have from 0 to 7 pips on each half? Explain how you found your answer.

3. How many pips in all are in a set of *double-three* dominoes? Explain.

4. How many pips in all are in a set of *double-seven* dominoes? Explain.

5. In the card game Mix and Match, players can trade in sets of three cards for extra points. There are three different cards in the game, each with a different pattern.

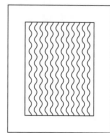 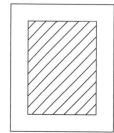 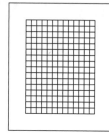

To trade in a set of three cards, a player must have three of one card (three alike) or one of each card (all different).

   a. How many different possible sets of three trade-in cards are there? Explain.

   b. Narciso claims that if you have five cards, you must be able to make a set to trade in for extra points. Do you agree with Narciso? Explain why or why not.

6. In how many different ways can three bows be chosen from a bag of four bows?

7. In how many different ways can three bows be chosen from a bag of six bows?

Investigation 5

Use these problems for additional practice after Investigation 5.

1. The computer in the children's library requires users to have a password consisting of two characters, such as Z9. Each character may be any letter or any digit, but no letter or digit can be repeated in the password.

   a. How many passwords are possible?

   b. How many more passwords could be used if repeating letters or digits were allowed? Explain your answer.

2. The local cafe sells ice cream sundaes that include 2 toppings. There are 12 toppings to choose from. How many combinations of two *different* toppings are possible?

3. The Megalopolis computer system requires users to have a password that contains at least four characters and no more than six characters, such as A1744K and A174. A character can be either a letter or a number, and letters and numbers may be repeated in a password.

   a. How many passwords are possible on this system? Show how you found your answer.

   b. Suppose a computer hacker tries to break into the system. The hacker writes a program that can generate and test 10^6 passwords of four to six characters per second. At this rate, how long would it take the hacker to test every possible password?

4. Many people who use automated teller machine (ATM) cards for banking must remember a four-digit personal identification number (PIN).

   a. If each digit in a four-digit PIN is a number from 0 to 9, how many possible four-digit PINs are there?

   b. A large bank has 76,500 customers who have ATM cards. Each of these cards has a four-digit PIN. Do you think that some customers have the same PIN? Why or why not?